MELODIC PERCEPTION

A PROGRAM FOR SELF-INSTRUCTION

MELODIC PERCEPTION

A PROGRAM FOR SELF-INSTRUCTION

James C. Carlsen, Ph.D.
Assistant Professor of Music
The University of Connecticut

McGRAW-HILL BOOK COMPANY

New York   St. Louis   San Francisco   Toronto   London   Sydney

II

One of the prime objectives of music training is to improve a learner's ability to listen to music perceptively. Such a skill implies a cognitive understanding of musical sound. Cognitive perception involves the ability to organize, either mentally or visibly, the symbols which represent the various elements of musical sound. Thus instruction aimed toward the development of aural perception skills must be chiefly concerned with relating the sound to the appropriate symbol.

In the learning of a nonverbal skill such as melodic perception, it is generally felt that practice or drill is intrinsic to the learning task. Because of individual differences, the amount of such practice will vary from person to person and from concept to concept. As a result, an instructional program in melodic perception should be an optimal one that basically does two things: (1) establishes procedures for cognitively perceiving aural stimuli and (2) provides musical materials with which these perception procedures can be practiced. This book and its companion recorded materials have been designed to accomplish these two requirements.

OBJECTIVES

The objectives of this course of study are to help the learner develop an ability to (1) write in accurate musical notation melodies which are played on different melodic instruments; (2) recognize when, and in what way, the printed music differs from that which is played; and (3) identify a performing instrument when it is playing a solo melody or rhythmic line. In addition, this course of study provides the learner with guidelines for practice in sight singing.

This course of study is designed in such a way that the learner can reach these objectives at his own pace and with a minimum of assistance from the instructor. This book is not a workbook in the usual sense of the word, because the learner is not graded on the answers he writes in the book. Rather, this is a book containing learning materials organized in a special way referred to as *programmed instruction*.

In addition to the self-pacing and self-instructional nature of these materials, three other characteristics will be noted: (1) information in the form of melodic elements is presented in steps (called frames) leading from the known to the unknown; (2) the learner is required to make a written response (usually in musical notation) to nearly all the items of information presented; and (3) the learner is provided immediate knowledge of the accuracy or inaccuracy of his response.

DEVELOPMENT OF THE MATERIALS

Programmed material of this sort is the product of many authors—the one whose name appears on the cover of the book and the students who provide him with responses which guide revision. This particular program was first tested on one student, revised, retested on another student, revised again, and group tested with the first-year music theory class at Northwestern University, Evanston, Illinois. On the basis of this testing and on the basis of further use at the University of Connecticut, the program has been revised a third time for its present form.

Evidence of its effectiveness to reach the objectives cited above is found in the field testing results. One group, working only with the programmed text and tape recorded materials over a period of nine weeks, reduced their mean error score on a criterion test by approximately 44 per cent. Another group, using the same program as supplementary material in first-year harmony for a period of 26 weeks, reduced their mean error score by approximately 65 per cent.

PREREQUISITES

In order to use this book effectively, the learner should (1) know the major key signatures through five sharps and five flats, (2) be able to read both G (treble) and F (bass) clefs, and (3) know rhythmic note values. In addition, he should have had experience in either playing a musical instrument or singing. The learner also should be able to write the various musical symbols legibly and accurately. However, a lack of notational ability can be overcome quickly by the perceptive person. Toward this end, the learner should notate all responses exactly as indicated in the printed music in the book. The value of this programmed approach can only be received by following each step exactly as instructed and in the sequence presented.

ACKNOWLEDGMENTS

This course of study would not have been possible had it not been for the contributions of many. I have already mentioned the students who participated in the initial experiments.

I am deeply indebted to Frank B. Cookson, Dean of the School of Fine Arts, University of Connecticut, for his encouragement and critical evaluation of these materials, both in their development at Northwestern University and in the revision for their present form. Many helpful suggestions were made by Professors Clifton Burmeister, Myles Friedman, and Hazel Nohavec Morgan when the idea of this program was being born. Professor Betty Kanable provided invaluable assistance during the experiment with these materials.

I also want to thank the staff of the School of Music at Northwestern University for their cooperation and support during the initial stage of the program's development and the music department faculties at Whitworth College and the University of Connecticut for their suggestions and encouragement during the preparation of these materials for publication.

Grateful acknowledgment is due those who cooperated in preparing the master tapes of the recorded material: Anton Kuskin, flute; Anton Swensen, clarinet; Brian Klitz, bassoon; John Thompson, trumpet; Barry Benjamin, horn; George Masso, trombone; Jack Heller, violin; Bruno DiCecco, cello; Leonard Seeber, piano; Robert Sherago, recording engineer; radio station WTIC, Hartford, Connecticut; and the Audio Visual Center, the University of Connecticut.

Finally, I want to thank Mary, my wife, and my children, Philip, Douglas, Susan and Kristine, for their encouragement, help, and patient forbearance during the writing of this book.

James C. Carlsen

TABLE OF CONTENTS

THE PROGRAMMED BOOK

1. Begin with Frame 1 at the top of page 1, covering the answer column with a mask (a sheet of paper or a 5- by 8-inch index card will do).
2. Do *exactly* what you are instructed to do in each frame.
3. Slide the mask down and compare your response with the correct answer printed in the right-hand column.
4. Continue down the page in this manner and proceed to the next page. (Slip the mask in and cover the page before turning to it in order to avoid seeing the answer to the next frame.)

THE PROGRAMMED TAPES

1. Obtain the first tape reel of recorded materials, place it on the tape player, and set the index counter on the machine at zero.
2. Listen to the tape when the book instructs you to press PLAY.
3. The tapes contain multiple presentations of most frames (the number in parenthesis in each frame indicates how many presentations of that frame are on the tape). After each presentation there will be a short period of silence on the tape.
4. Stop the tape after each presentation. Think through what you have heard and write the response required if possible. If you need another hearing, press PLAY. Do not let the tape "play through" while you are writing your response. *Always* stop the machine after each presentation.
5. The first presentation in each frame will contain a voice identification of the frame number. If you are not ready to proceed to that particular frame, rewind the tape for additional hearings of the frame on which you are working. Listen as often as you find necessary. However, attempt to complete your response in as few hearings as possible and with a minimum of time in between, since most test-item melodies will be presented only three times.
6. If there are more presentations than you need, you may advance the tape to the next

frame (this may take a little practice) or you may play through all presentations for the additional practice they provide.

7. Most frames will begin with a tonic triad which identifies the tonal center of the melody to follow. This will be followed by two measures in which the metric beat is counted. After this, the instrument will play. Always begin your conducting of the beats on the second measure of the introductory metric count. (See item 4 of the General Procedures that follow.)

GENERAL PROCEDURES

1. If your listening session should end before finishing a reel of tape, make note of the number showing on the index counter on the frame which you are studying. This will make it easier to locate that frame on the tape at your next session.

2. Since you may listen to each frame as many times as you desire, do not allow yourself to look at the correct answer until you are completely certain that your written response is correct.

3. If your response should be incorrect, draw a mark through it at the point or points of error and write it correctly on manuscript paper. On the self-analysis charts at the end of the book, indicate the frame number and the nature of the error. For example:

SELF-ANALYSIS CHART
Sec. III, Frames 118 to 166

FRAME	NATURE OF ERROR	REMARKS
130	♪♪ written as ♩ ♪	listen more carefully for durations and rests in compound meter

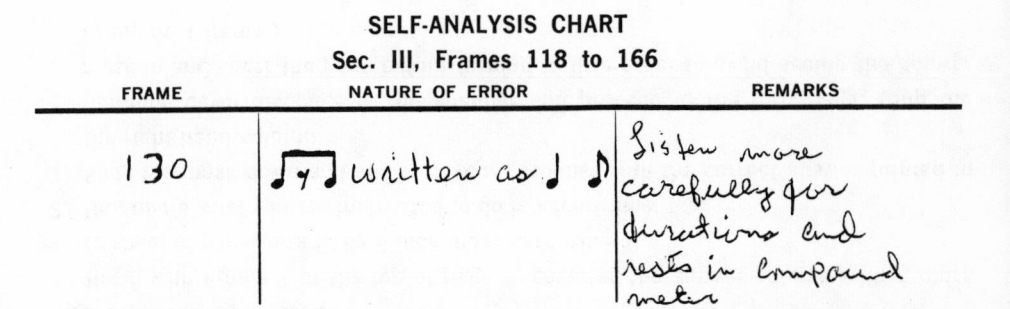

Do not bypass this procedure. **Doing so will lessen the effectiveness of this program of study.**

It is recommended that you use the conductor beat patterns for this (see illustrations on page 215). *It is important that you make some physical response of this sort while you listen to the recorded material.*

5. Sing all melodies, even if a frame does not contain that instruction. Sing mentally (to yourself) rather than aloud.

REVIEW PROCEDURES

Developing aural perception is an additive process. Elements first learned, stepwise motion, for example, are constantly being reinforced because they continually recur in more complex settings. For this reason, specific review frames are not included in this program. On the other hand, there are many frames which are included to provide additional practice possibility.

Review should occur when:

1. You make errors on two successive frames
2. You find it necessary to listen to frames several more times than the tape provides
3. You finish a section and are preparing to take the test.

Use your self-analysis charts for guidance in reviewing. By using the following suggestions, the book and tapes can provide additional practice as well as review.

1. Determine the section to be reviewed or practiced and obtain the tape reel for those frames.
2. Read your analysis remarks about problems in that section.
3. Cover the original response with your mask, except for the clef, key signature, and meter signature.
4. Use that frame as a completion response and write the entire melody on a separate sheet of manuscript paper.
5. Follow the correction procedure outlined in item 3 of the General Procedures.
6. For additional review at a still later date, use the incorrect responses you have made on manuscript paper for error-detection purposes.

An *index* to the frames in which all concepts are first introduced is provided in the back of the book.

MELODIC PERCEPTION

A PROGRAM FOR SELF-INSTRUCTION

1 Press PLAY

A melody has two basic elements. One element is pitch,

 (1)

and the other is duration of tone, or rhythm.

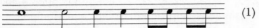 (1)

The performing instrument is *clarinet*. (For the first portion of the program, the instrument playing the example will be indicated.)

ANSWER

No written response required. Proceed to the next frame.

---

2 Press PLAY

The first element of melody which was mentioned was pitch.

When musical pitches are put together in some form of organization, the result is referred to as a melodic line. Listen to the following simple organization of musical pitches. It constitutes a melodic line.

 (1)

The performing instrument is *violin*. Be particularly attentive to the distinguishing quality of sound made by each instrument.

ANSWER

No written response required. Proceed to the next frame.

3 Press PLAY

The second element of melody which was mentioned was rhythm. Because of the importance of rhythm to melody, the first part of this course of study will deal only with rhythmic perception. For the time being, the rhythmic line played in each frame will be on one pitch.

Some sort of physical response has been found helpful in developing rhythmic understanding. This would be a good time to develop your conductor beat patterns,* but if you prefer, you may tap the beat with your hand. Whichever you do, do vigorously.

Conduct the beats which are located by the arrows while you listen to this rhythmic line.

 (1)

The performing instrument is *horn*. (Yes, it is a *French* horn, but most musicians refer to it simply as *horn*.)

*For an illustration of the conductor beat patterns needed for this course of study, see page 215.

ANSWER

At the beginning of each frame, the tempo will be established by counting two complete measures of the metric beats. Begin conducting on the second of these measures before the instrument begins to play. Proceed to the next frame.

4 Press PLAY

Perhaps you noticed that the beats which you conducted in the preceding frame had a consistent duration and grouped themselves into patterns of four. This grouping was made obvious to the eye by the use of bar lines.

This grouping of beats of consistent duration is referred to as the *meter*. Because there were four beats in each group in the preceding frame, we would refer to that pattern as *quadruple* meter.

In this frame, the rhythmic line has a different grouping of beats. Conduct the beats while you listen.

 (1)

Because this rhythmic line's beats are grouped in threes, we would call this triple
_____. The performing instrument is *cello*.

ANSWER

meter

5 Press PLAY

This frame contains rhythmic notation which can be grouped into patterns of two beats. Listen to this line in duple meter, conducting the beats while you listen.

After you have listened to the line played once, stop the machine and put in the bar lines to make the printed line correspond to the duple meter signature, that is, .

 (2)

ANSWER

The performing instrument is *flute*.

Your bar lines should have been at the places indicated by the brackets. If you have made an error in your placement of the bar lines, rewrite them correctly.

As you listen to this rhythmic line played again, notice particularly how the beats can be felt in groups of two. After you have listened, sing the rhythmic line as you conduct the beats.

Press PLAY

---

6 Press PLAY

It is obvious that music contains notes whose duration may be shorter than, longer than, or the same as, the metric beats. The different durations of notes heard create patterns. These patterns are referred to as *rhythm*.

Listen to the two lines in this frame. The first has a rhythm which is the same as the meter. The rhythm of the second line is different from the meter but fits on the meter. The performing instrument is *clarinet*.

 (1)

(1)

Duple, triple, or quadruple meter refers to the number of beats in a measure. These lines are both in _____ meter.

ANSWER

quadruple

7 Press PLAY

When you hear the count "1-2-3-4-1-2-3-4" you are hearing a vocal presentation of quadruple meter. For duple meter the count would be "1-2-1-2." This grouping of beats of consistent duration is called the meter.

When you hear this line:

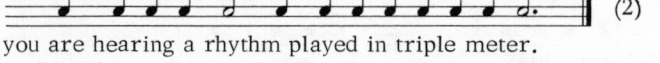 (2)

you are hearing a rhythm played in triple meter.

Stop the machine and put in the appropriate meter signature and bar lines to make it correspond to triple meter.

ANSWER

The performing instrument is *piano*.

Meter signature and bar lines should have been at the places indicated by the brackets. If you have made an error in your placement of the bar lines, rewrite them correctly.

As you listen to this rhythmic line played again, notice particularly how the beats can be felt in groups of three. After you have listened, sing the rhythmic line as you conduct the beats.

Press PLAY

---

8 Press PLAY

Rhythm patterns frequently divide the metric beats into parts (notes) of shorter duration. If the beat is divided into two parts, *simple meter* is the result. If the beat is divided into three parts, the result is *compound meter*. For the time being, attention will be focused on simple meter.

Conduct the beat located by the arrows while you listen to this example of simple meter. Notice how the eighth note beams bind the eighth notes into groups of two.

 (1)

The performing instrument is *trombone*.

ANSWER

No written response required. Proceed to the next frame.

9 Do NOT press PLAY until you have read the instructions.
A conductor beat pattern physically describes the meter. The pattern provides a good basis for perceiving the rhythm. For this reason, *always* conduct the metric beat when listening to the melodic or the rhythmic lines in this program of study.

In this frame, mark an arrow above the notes where each beat occurs. Because this rhythmic line is in duple meter, make certain that you have two beats indicated for each measure.

Do not press PLAY until you have checked your response with the correct answer.

After checking your answer, correct it if necessary. This rhythmic line is recorded twice on the tape. The performing instrument is *trumpet*. Conduct a duple beat pattern along with the first presentation.

Sing the rhythmic line along with the second presentation while continuing to conduct the meter.

Press PLAY

---

10 *Always* examine the meter signature *before* listening to the instruments play the recorded material for each frame. Ask yourself:
1. How many beats are indicated for each measure?
2. What kind of a note is to receive a metric beat?

In this frame, place arrows above the notes where the metric beat occurs. Some notes will have more than one arrow above them because their duration will be more than one metric beat.

Do not press PLAY until after you have made your response and checked your answer with the one in the answer column.

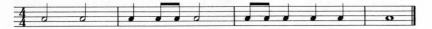

If you made an error, try to determine the nature of the error and why you made it. After correcting it, listen to the two presentations of this rhythmic line on the tape, and:
1. Conduct the beat *both* times.
2. Sing *and* conduct the second time.

The performing instrument is *bassoon*.

Press PLAY

11a Indicate with arrows the location of the beats in this rhythmic line. Do not press PLAY yet; first check your answer.

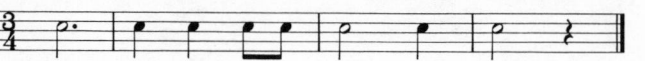

ANSWER

Any errors? If so, proceed to the next frame *now*.

If you made no error, you are to conduct and sing the above rhythmic line as it is played. It will be played twice. The performing instrument is *horn*.

Press PLAY

After listening, proceed to Frame 12.

11b The purpose in having you put arrows over the note where a beat occurs is to focus your attention on the meter which serves as a framework for the rhythmic pattern(s).

In this rhythmic line you have only one note in the first measure, but at the same time, you have a grouping of three beats of equal duration.

As you conduct a triple meter pattern along with the playing of this line, observe how your arm describes three distinct beats while only the first note is being played. Sing the rhythm along with the second presentation.

Press PLAY

The performing instrument is *horn*.

ANSWER

No written response required. Proceed to the next frame.

12 Press PLAY

Probably the easiest rhythm to recognize aurally is one which is the same as the meter.

In the next few frames, a section of the rhythmic pattern will be omitted from the printed music. Conduct the metric beat* while you listen.

The omitted section can be completed with a rhythm pattern which is the same as the meter. Complete the omitted measure by writing the rhythm played by the cello for that measure.

 (2)

The performing instrument is *cello*.

*To conduct the metric beat means using the conducting pattern appropriate to the meter.

ANSWER

If you had other than four quarter notes, your answer could not be the "same as the meter," since the meter in this rhythmic line is notated in groups of four quarter notes. Sing *and* conduct the rhythmic line that was played.

---

13 The problem in this frame is similar to that in the preceding one. Complete the omitted measure.

Press PLAY

 (2)

The performing instrument is *piano*.

ANSWER

If your answer was incorrect, follow the printed rhythmic line above while you listen to it played once more. You may have to rewind the tape a short distance in order to do this.

After you have sung this rhythmic line, proceed to the next frame.

14 In addition to notes which are of the *same* duration as the metric beat, rhythmic patterns may also use notes which are of *longer* duration.

In this frame, the omitted section will contain a note of longer duartion than one metric beat. It will also contain notes which are of the same duration as the metric beats.

Examine the meter signature. Make sure that your response contains the accurate number of metric beats. Complete the omitted measure.

Press PLAY

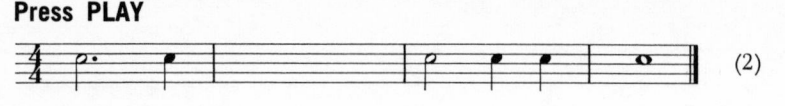 (2)

The performing instrument is *violin*.

ANSWER

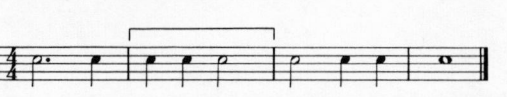

If you are conducting the metric beats, you observed that the third note of the omitted measure received two beats. Play this frame again if you made an error.

---

15 This frame omits two measures from the beginning of the printed music. The measures will require notes which are longer than, and notes which are the same as, the duration of the metric beats.

Press PLAY

 (2)

The performing instrument is *trombone*.

ANSWER

---

16 Complete the omitted section of this rhythmic line. Conduct the metric beat as you listen.

Press PLAY

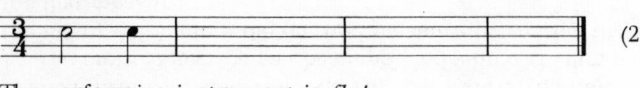 (2)

The performing instrument is *flute*.

ANSWER

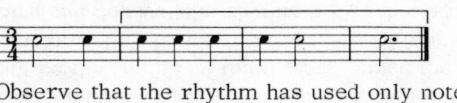

Observe that the rhythm has used only notes the same as or longer than the metric beat.

17 Press PLAY

In Frame 8 it was said that rhythm patterns frequently divide the metric beats into parts (notes) of shorter duration.

In order to perceive rhythms involving divided beats, it is necessary to feel the division. This feeling can be aided by the use of a physical response which corresponds to the regular division of the beat.

With one hand, conduct the metric beat indicated by the quarter notes and played by the horn. With the other hand, tap the division of these beats indicated by the eighth notes. The result will be two taps for each beat.

(1)

The performing instrument is *horn*.

---

18 Whenever you have printed music to follow such as you have in this frame, *always* examine the printed music *before* you listen.

In this frame, the printed music is the notation of a rhythmic line. Observe the meter. Observe where the metric beats will occur. Notice also the location of the divided beats.

Tap the divided beat indicated by the lower line of notes with one hand. With the other, conduct the metric beats. Do this while you listen to the clarinet play the upper line of notes.

Press PLAY

(1)

The performing instrument is *clarinet*.

19   *Before* listening,

1. Examine the meter signature.
2. Examine the printed music.

In this frame, the trumpet will play the rhythm indicated by the top notes, but will use different pitches to form a simple melodic line.

As the trumpet plays, conduct the beats and tap the divisions as you did with the clarinet in the preceding frame.

Press PLAY

 (1)

The performing instrument is *trumpet* .

ANSWER

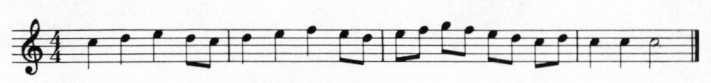

No written response required. Proceed to the next frame.

---

20   The procedure of tapping the divided beats and conducting the metric beats while listening to the recorded examples is an important one. You must continue to do this on *all* the frames which follow. This is necessary for the development of an "inner feeling" of the divided beat.

Follow the same procedure on this frame which you did on the preceding one, even though this frame does not contain the eighth-note indication of the divided beat.

Press PLAY

 (1)

The performing instrument is *bassoon* .

ANSWER

No written response required. Proceed to the next frame.

---

21   The omitted section in this frame can be completed with a rhythm pattern which is comprised entirely of divided beats.

Conduct the metric beat and tap the divided beat while you listen.

Press PLAY

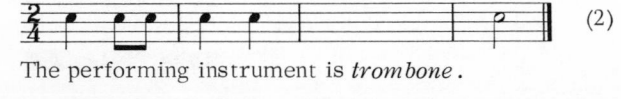 (2)

The performing instrument is *trombone* .

ANSWER

Since the book has discussed only the eighth-note division of beats, you might have expected the answer to be four eighth notes. Division of the beat into notes of even shorter duration will be taken up later in the program.

22 The omitted section in this frame contains notes which are shorter than the metric beat, as well as notes which are the same duration as the metric beat.

Conduct beats and tap divisions while you listen. Complete the omitted section.
Press PLAY

The performing instrument is *cello*.

ANSWER

(2)

Did you notice the similarity of rhythmic pattern in the first part of measures 2 and 3? More will be said later about repetition as an aid to aural perception.

---

23 Rhythm may be a combination of durations which are longer than, shorter than, or the same as the metric beat. The omitted section in this frame involves all three. Complete the omitted measure.
Press PLAY

The performing instrument is *flute*.

ANSWER

(2)

Sing what you heard played before proceeding to the next frame.

---

24 The rhythm in the omitted measures involves the three possibilities of duration which have been discussed. Conduct the metric beat and tap the divided beat while you listen. Complete the omitted section.
Press PLAY

(2)

The performing instrument is *violin*.

ANSWER

25 Following the same procedure, complete the three omitted measures in this frame.

Press PLAY

 (2)

The performing instrument is *horn*.

ANSWER

---

26 Press PLAY

A practical consideration for a musician is the ability to detect error in performance. This skill is of particular importance to the conductor.

In the next few frames, the printed rhythmic pattern will differ from that which you hear. Bracket the measure where the rhythmic difference occurs and write what you hear for that measure on the second staff, as in this example.

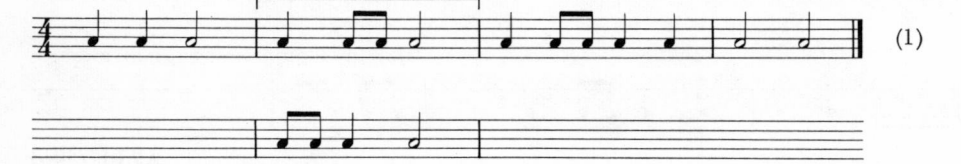 (1)

The performing instrument is *trumpet*.

ANSWER

No written response required. Proceed to the next frame.

27 The purpose of having you compare what you see with what you hear (correcting the differences) is to provide additional means for improving aural perception ability. It is not enough to be able to detect differences. The good musician must be able to tell the precise nature of the difference.

Before listening to this rhythmic line examine the meter signature and the printed music. The difference which you will hear in this frame will involve a note of longer duration than the metric beat. Locate the point of difference and write what you hear played.

Press PLAY

(2)

The performing instrument is *piano*.

ANSWER

After checking your answer, always sing the rhythmic line or melody as you heard it played. Do this before proceeding to the next frame. Use a conductor beat pattern and tap the divided beats while you sing.

---

28 Examining the printed music before listening makes it possible to obtain an idea of what you might expect to hear played. One of the best ways to accomplish this is to *sing mentally* the printed music as a part of the "examination" process.

Before listening to the recording of the rhythmic line on the tape, *sing* the printed response to yourself while conducting the metric beats and tapping the divided beats.

After you have done this, listen to the recorded rhythmic line and compare it with the printed one. Do not sing aloud while making the comparison—only follow the printed music and listen.

Locate and correct the differences as before.

Press PLAY

(2)

The performing instrument is *bassoon*.

ANSWER

You may have found the "presinging" of the rhythmic line to have been difficult. Your ability to do this will improve with practice. An important part of this practice is to *always* sing the rhythmic line printed in the answer column. This procedure is aided by the fact that you will have just heard it played. Be sure that you follow the printed music while singing.

29 Examine the meter signature and the printed music in this frame. Sing the rhythmic line before listening, as you did in the preceding frame. Remember: Do not sing aloud while making your comparison.

Locate and correct the differences as you did before.

Press PLAY

(2)

The performing instrument is *trombone.*

ANSWER

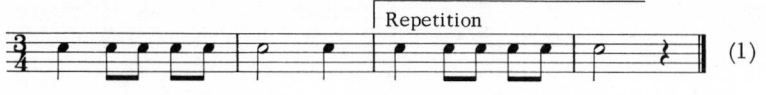

---

30 Press PLAY

In most instances, composers employ devices in their writing which will provide either unity or variety. One of the devices used to obtain a feeling of unity is the technique of *repetition.*

Listen to this rhythmic line and observe the repetition of the first measure played in the third.

(1)

The performing instrument is *clarinet.*

ANSWER

No written response required. Proceed to the next frame.

31 If you see a repetition in the printed music, the repetition should sound when the example is played. The opposite approach is equally valid. Whenever you hear a repetition in the selection played, make certain that it appears in the printed music.

Examine the printed music in this frame. Observe that it contains no printed rhythmic repetition. Mentally sing this rhythmic line before listening to the recorded example.

The cello will play a rhythmic repetition in its performance. Locate the repetition and write it in its proper measure on the second staff.

Press PLAY

(2)

The performing instrument is *cello*.

ANSWER

After correcting any errors which you have made, sing the corrected rhythm while conducting the metric beat and tapping the divided beat. Observe the effect of the repetitions as you sing.

---

32 The printed music in this frame contains a repeated rhythmic pattern. Listen for this repetition in the performance. If you do not hear a repetition played, you have detected an error.

Press PLAY

(2)

The performing instrument is *violin*.

ANSWER

There was no rhythmic repetition heard in this rhythmic line.

After correcting any errors you have made, sing the corrected rhythmic line before proceeding to the next frame.

33 Examine the meter signature and the printed music. Whenever you see rhythms written in repeated patterns as you do in this frame, set your mental ear to hear the repetition. This is helped if you mentally sing what you see printed before you listen.

If the repetition does not occur in performance as the printed music would indicate that it should, you have detected an error.

Indicate any differences that might exist between the performance and the printed music in this frame.

Press PLAY

(2)

The performing instrument is *trombone*.

ANSWER

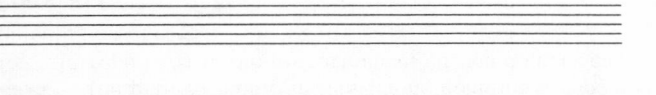

They did sound the same! If you made a correction, go back and listen to this frame again. Otherwise, proceed to the next frame.

---

34 The use of repetition in this frame is similar to that in the preceding one. Tap and conduct as previously instructed for divided beats.

Press PLAY

(2)

The performing instrument is *flute*.

ANSWER

Did you observe that measure 3 was a repetition of measure 1 in the example which you heard? This awareness of repetition is one of the perception skills which you are developing at this point.

After singing the correct rhythmic line, proceed to the next frame.

35 It was stated earlier that composers use different devices in their writing to obtain either unity or variety. If repetition aids the feeling of unity, the composer would probably avoid repetition if he were intent upon obtaining variety.

In this frame, neither the printed music nor the performance contains a repetition. Locate and correct the rhythmic difference as before.

Press PLAY

 (2)

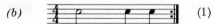

The performing instrument is *horn*.

Tapping the divided beats helps to make obvious the differences when they involve notes of shorter duration than the metric beat.

---

36 Press PLAY

A dot after a note adds one-half the value of the note. You probably already knew this, but listen to the effect when you hear it. Listen to *a*:

(a)  (1)

You heard a rhythm which was the same as the meter. Now listen to *b*:

(b)  (1)

This time the rhythm was different from the meter. The first note was held for two beats. To have a note held for three beats could be done with a tie between a half note and a quarter note, as indicated in *c*:

(c) 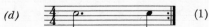 (1)

Another way to indicate a three-beat note is with a dotted note, as in *d*:

(d) (1)

The performing instrument is *clarinet*.

ANSWER

No written response required. Proceed to the next frame.

37 **Press PLAY**

Listen to this line. The performing instrument is *trumpet*.

 (1)

Rewrite this rhythm on the staff below, using dotted notes instead of tied notes.

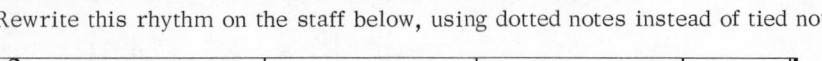

ANSWER

The brackets indicate the places where you should have written dotted quarter notes.

---

38 Before listening to this rhythmic line, examine the meter signature and the printed music. Sing the first line containing the tied notes.

Rewrite the rhythmic line with dotted notes on the second staff. After you have done this, check your response for accuracy.

Do not press PLAY until you have checked your written response with the correct answer.

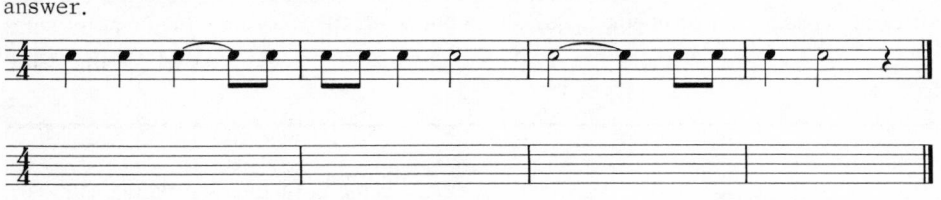

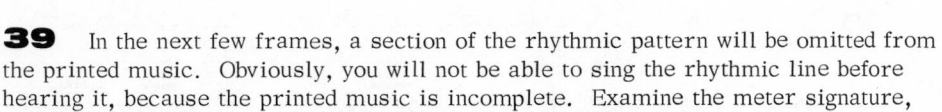

ANSWER

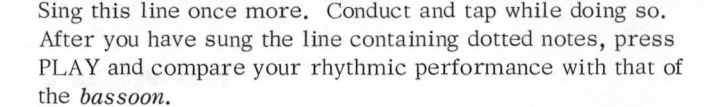

Sing this line once more. Conduct and tap while doing so. After you have sung the line containing dotted notes, press PLAY and compare your rhythmic performance with that of the *bassoon*.

---

39 In the next few frames, a section of the rhythmic pattern will be omitted from the printed music. Obviously, you will not be able to sing the rhythmic line before hearing it, because the printed music is incomplete. Examine the meter signature, however, and that portion of the music which is printed.

Conduct and tap while you listen. After you have heard the pattern once or twice, sing it to yourself. This will help you remember it.

Complete the omitted measure. Use a dotted note rather than tied notes.

Press PLAY

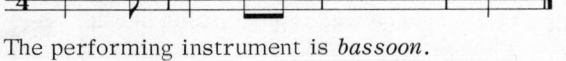 (2)

The performing instrument is *bassoon*.

ANSWER

Did you hear measure 3 as a repetition of measure 1? Sing this rhythmic line while conducting the metric beat and tapping the divided beat. After you have done this, proceed to the next frame.

40 In this frame, the rhythmic pattern in the omitted measure is repeated later in the rhythmic line. Complete the omitted measure.

Press PLAY

 (2)

The performing instrument is *cello*.

ANSWER

---

41 No two measures in this rhythmic line are alike. Your response should include notes longer than, shorter than, and the same as, the metric beat. Conduct and tap while you listen. Complete the omitted measure.

Press PLAY

 (2)

The performing instrument is *flute*.

ANSWER

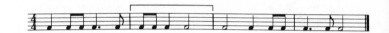

42a Being able to sing a line after hearing it only once or twice indicates a use of tonal and rhythmic memory. To a large extent, such memory depends upon practice.

Tonal and rhythmic memory practice can be obtained on the frames in this book which omit all or a portion of the printed music. In such frames, listen to the instrument play the line and then immediately sing it to yourself.

Listen for repetition in the rhythmic line in this frame. One of the omitted measures will be exactly like one of the printed ones. Complete the omitted section.

Press PLAY

 (3)

The performing instrument is *violin*.

ANSWER

If you made an error in this frame, or if you had to listen to more than three presentations, proceed to Frame 42b *now*.

If you wrote a correct response in three presentations or less, sing the rhythmic line while conducting the beat, then skip to Frame 43.

42b   Rewind the tape now and listen to one presentation of Frame 42a.

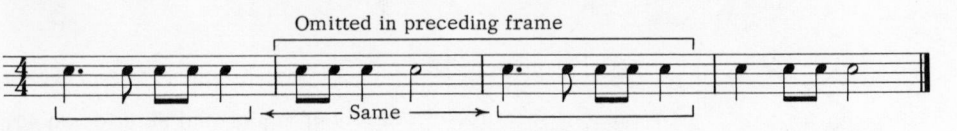

In the rhythmic line which you just heard, measure 3 should have sounded to you exactly like measure 1. Because of this, you needed only to *copy* in measure 3 what you could see printed in measure 1. This procedure makes it possible to focus your attention on the nonrepeated material of measure 2. This procedure is a general one, which can be followed in any frame involving repetition in the response.

Sing this line while conducting the beat. After you have done this, turn to Frame 43 for another similar rhythmic problem.

ANSWER

No written response required. Proceed to the next frame.

---

43   Repetition and dotted rhythm are involved in your response to this frame. Complete the omitted section.

Press PLAY

(3)

The performing instrument is *horn.*

ANSWER

Are you tapping the divided beat while you listen? This is as important as conducting the metric beat when the music involves notes which are shorter in duration than the metric beats. Incidentally, most music does involve divided beats.

If you have made an error, rewind the tape and listen again to this rhythmic line. Sing the rhythmic line before proceeding to the next frame.

44 You cannot always depend upon repetition for help. Here is a rhythmic line with no two measures alike. Sing this line to yourself after one hearing if possible. Use more if necessary. Complete the missing sections.

Press PLAY

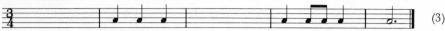

The performing instrument is *piano*.

(3)

ANSWER

Notice that the omitted sections were the same rhythms omitted from the preceding frame. If you made an error, relisten to Frame 44.

Sing this rhythmic line while conducting the metric beat before proceeding to the next frame.

---

45 **Press PLAY**

It was stated earlier that when musical pitches are put together in some form of organization, the result is referred to as a melodic line. Listen to this organization of pitches. It constitutes a melodic line.

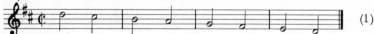

(1)

This melodic line played by the *trumpet* might be simply called a D major scale. It could also be called a rhythmic line, because it contains notes whose durations create a pattern—in this case, a steady pattern due to the consistency of duration of each note.

Note: In this frame and the next, a half note (♩) will be used as the metric beat.

ANSWER

No written response required. Proceed to the next frame.

---

46 **Press PLAY**

A scale-like melody with all notes of equal duration seems to lack rhythmic interest. Listen to this D major scale again.

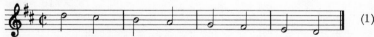

(1)

Listen again to the same scale, but now with a different pattern of note durations.

(1)

With that rhythmic change, you easily recognize the melody as *Joy to the World*.

The performing instrument again is *trumpet*.

ANSWER

No written response required. Proceed to the next frame.

47 The next few frames will contain melodies which are rhythmic adaptations of major scales. For the time being, these melodies will begin and end on the tonic. Any change of direction within the melody will occur on the tonic.

In the next few frames, the melodies which you will hear will differ from the printed ones. Bracket the measure where the rhythmic difference occurs. On the second staff, write what you hear for that measure, as indicated in this example.

Press PLAY

(1)

Your response should contain clef, meter signature, and correct notations. Without a clef, it is impossible to indicate pitches.

ANSWER

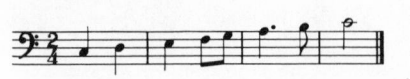

Remember to sing the printed music to yourself *before* listening.

After you have listened to the *trombone*, and you have made your written response, sing the melody *again*. If you are in a location where you can sing aloud, select an octave register within your range. Do not try to sing in the same octave register as the instrument playing, unless that register is a comfortable one for you.

---

48 Until now, you have been (1) examining the meter signature and (2) examining the printed music (which included singing mentally the rhythmic line), before listening to the recorded performance of that line.

Now that pitches have been introduced, it is important also to examine the *key signature* before listening to the recorded performance. Mentally locate the *tonic* (sometimes referred to as "1" or "do") on the staff.

Conduct the metric beat and tap the divided beat while you listen to this frame.

Bracket and correct the rhythmic difference in this melodic line. The difference involves dotted rhythms.

Press PLAY

(2)

The performing instrument is *clarinet.*

ANSWER

Your answer should have contained the G clef and the key signature, in addition to the corrected rhythm.

You have observed by this time that a dot after a note lengthens that note. As a result, the note following is delayed. This feeling of delay can serve as a useful aid in detecting dotted rhythms.

49 Examine the meter and the *key* signatures. Observe that the printed music begins on the tonic (or "1" or "do").

Before listening to the cello play its melody, sing the printed melody. Do not be concerned about starting this scalewise melody on the correct initial pitch. It is important, however, that you sing the correct rhythm.

After you have done the above procedures, compare the recorded melody with the printed one. There will be two points of rhythmic difference. One of the differences will involve rhythmic repetition and the other the feeling of delay as a result of a dotted rhythm. Locate both points and correct.

Press PLAY

(3)

The performing instrument is *cello*.

Did you add the clef and key signature? Conduct and tap while you sing this melody.

---

50 This frame also contains two points of difference. One involves divided beats and repetitions. The other involves dotted rhythm.

Press PLAY

(3)

The performing instrument is *piano*.

51 Two adjoining measures will contain rhythmic differences. Locate and correct.

Press PLAY

(3)

The performing instrument is *bassoon*.

ANSWER

Your clue to the correct response should have been obtained from the rhythmic repetition. Conduct, tap the divided beats, and sing this melody before proceeding to the next frame.

---

52 In the next few frames, a portion of the printed music will be omitted. As a result, you will not be able to sing the melodies before hearing them played.

You can examine other aspects of the printed music such as the meter signature the key signature, and the portions of the melody which are printed. It is important to do these things *before listening*.

After you have heard the melody played once or twice, sing it to yourself before making your written response.

All melodic motion thus far has been stepwise. Interval skips will not be introduced until later. Rhythmic repetition is involved in this frame.

Press PLAY

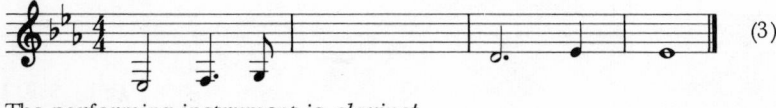

(3)

The performing instrument is *clarinet*.

ANSWER

Notice that no departure from ascending or descending major scales has occurred. For a time, only rhythmic adaptations of major scales will be heard. This means that the melodies will begin and end on the tonic note.

53 Examine the key signature and mentally locate where the tonic will be on the staff. Because only rhythmic adaptations of major scales are being used at present, examination of the printed music indicates that the omitted measure can be completed with two notes. Complete the omitted measure.

Press PLAY

 (2)

The performing instrument is *flute*.

ANSWER

Your ability to hear accurately is improved in direct proportion to the amount of information you are able to get from the printed music before you listen.

---

54 Even before listening to this melody, the printed music provides you with certain helpful information.

In this frame, you are to indicate the number of the item of information which the printed music does *not* provide:
1. Number of metric beats in a measure
2. Location of tonic
3. Number of pitches needed to complete a major scale
4. Rhythm of the omitted section

The performing instrument is *horn*.

Complete the omitted measures.

Press PLAY

 (3)

The printed music does not provide the information stated in item 1, 2, 3, or 4. (Draw a circle around the correct number.)

ANSWER

The printed music does not provide the information stated in item 4.

55 In this frame, the printed line contains only the meter and key signatures, the bar lines, and an indication of the first pitch.

After listening to the violin play the melody once or twice, sing it to yourself. If you are able to do this, you can then mentally hear the melody as often as necessary to make the correct response. If your response is correct, you will know that your tonal and rhythmic memory are good.

Press PLAY

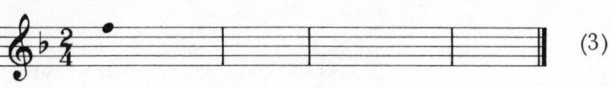 (3)

The performing instrument is *violin*.

ANSWER

Even though your response may have been correct, sing the melody to yourself after you have completed and checked your response. Use another playing of the recorded melody if necessary to check yourself.

---

56 Because the last note of this melody is indicated, you should not have trouble locating the starting note. Complete the melody.

Press PLAY

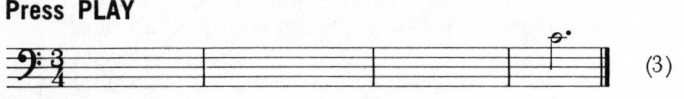 (3)

The performing instrument is *trombone*.

ANSWER

---

57 This frame contains no rhythmic repetition. Write the melody you hear.

Press PLAY

 (3)

The performing instrument is *trumpet*.

ANSWER

Continue to sing these melodies to yourself, both before you write your response and again after you have checked your response.

58 Write this cello melody.

Press PLAY

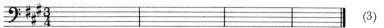

(3)

The performing instrument is *cello*.

ANSWER

---

59 The melody in this frame contains neither new rhythmic nor new pitch concepts.

Press PLAY

(3)

The performing instrument is *piano*.

ANSWER

If your answer was correct, you probably noted two principal points: (1) The melody consisted of an ascending and descending major scale; (2) measures 3 and 4 were a rhythmic repetition of measures 1 and 2. Conduct and tap while you sing this melody.

---

60 Until this frame, the following note values in simple meter have been used:

Beginning with this frame, attention will be given to developing perception of rests. In the next few frames the following rests will be found in the melodies. Beside each rest is its related note value.

Conduct and tap while you listen. Complete the missing measure.

Press PLAY

(3)

The performing instrument is *bassoon*.

ANSWER

If your answer was correct, you probably observed that the rest occurred at a place in the measure that is normally accented. The absence of a note at this place should have made the rest obvious.

61 Rests do not always occur on an accented portion of the measure. When they do not, it is necessary to determine precisely when the performing instrument *ceases* to sound, in order to locate the beginning of the rest.

In this frame, the trumpet plays only one note in the first measure and four in the second. After hearing this melody played once or twice, sing it to yourself. Be careful to perform the rests in your singing in the same manner you heard them performed in the played version. Complete the omitted measures.

Press PLAY

(3)

The performing instrument is *trumpet*.

ANSWER

If you had difficulty detecting that the sound of the first note ended precisely at the beginning of count 4, listen again to this melody while conducting and tapping.

Sing this melody again now. Observe the rest in measure 1.

62 The omitted section in this frame contains a combination of two rests (one immediately following the other) and involves rhythmic repetitions.

Conduct and tap while you listen. Sing the melody to yourself before making your response.

Press PLAY

(3)

The performing instrument is *clarinet*.

ANSWER

Observe that the combination of the two rests in the third measure corresponds rhythmically to the dotted quarter note in the second. Listen to this melody again if necessary.

63 Tapping the divided beat will be of help in determining the rests in this frame. Listen for the precise point when the cello ceases to sound its first note in the second measure.

Press PLAY

(3)

The performing instrument is *cello*.

ANSWER

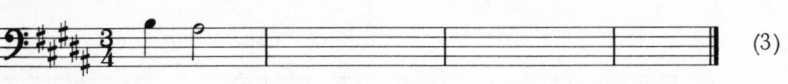

Be certain that the rests were in the correct order. Rests are usually placed to correspond with the metric beat as in the melody above.

64 Complete this melody. A rest is involved.

Press PLAY

 (3)

The performing instrument is *flute*.

ANSWER

The rest in this frame is more easily detected if you tap the divided beat.

When singing, be very careful to observe the rests precisely.

---

65 Rests are involved in two of the omitted measures in this frame.

Press PLAY

 (3)

The performing instrument is *horn*.

ANSWER

---

66 In the following few frames, the melodies will have at least two measures containing rests. One of the measure's rests will differ in duration in performance from that printed.

Before listening to the recorded melodies, examine the meter signature and the key signature. After you have determined the number of beats for each measure and the location of the tonic, examine the printed music.

Sing what you see printed, paying particular attention to the duration of both notes and rests.

After you have listened to the *violin* play this melody, compare what you see (and sang) with what you heard. Bracket the measure where the difference occurs and write on the second staff what you heard played for that measure.

Press PLAY

 (2)

ANSWER

The crescendo on the first note in the third measure should have made the duration obvious. Having observed this you needed only to detect the precise ending location to determine the rest which was needed. *Note:* It was not necessary to indicate the crescendo in your response. If you did, you are listening well.

67   From the remarks in the preceding frame, it would appear that rests are most easily determined by:

1. Detecting the precise ending of the preceding note
2. Detecting the precise beginning of the following note

Apply these two procedures in this frame.

Press PLAY

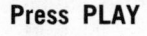

(2)

The performing instrument is *trombone*.

ANSWER

If you were conducting the beat, it should not have been difficult to determine that the first note in the second measure began on beat 2 rather than beat 3. Tapping the divided beat should help identify it as a dotted rhythm.

---

68   After examining the printed music and "presinging" the melody you see there, listen to the *trumpet* melody and compare the two. Bracket and rewrite as before.

Press PLAY

(2)

ANSWER

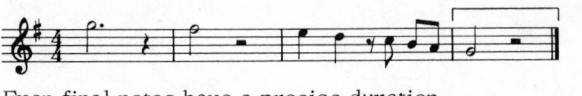

Even final notes have a precise duration.

   Conduct and tap while you sing this melody. Sustain the final note for its full duration but no more. Listen to the recording again to check your accuracy.

TEST 1

Before proceeding with the program, complete the test items for Test 1, which will be found at the back of the book. Obtain the tape-recorded materials for this test from your instructor.

69 **Press PLAY**

The melodies in the preceding frames have continued either up or down to the tonic before changing direction. In the following frames, most of the melodies will contain changes of direction on other scale degrees, as well as the tonic.

Conduct and tap while listening to this melody played by the *flute*. It changes melodic direction twice. Both changes are on notes other than the tonic.

 (1)

ANSWER

No written response required. Proceed to the next frame.

---

70 **Press PLAY**

In simple meter, the rhythmic point of direction change can occur in two places. In one, the change is heard on the *accented* portion of a beat, as in this example:

 (1)

The second place where direction change can be heard is on an *unaccented* portion of a beat, as in this example:

 (1)

The performing instrument is *piano*.

ANSWER

No written response required. Proceed to the next frame.

71 The printed music in the responses of the next few frames provide only the rhythmic notation of the melodies played. You are to place an arrow over the note in the rhythmic notation where you hear the change of melodic direction occur, as in this example.

Conduct and tap while you listen. After listening to the melody once or twice, sing it precisely as you heard it. If you can do this, you will be able to slow the tempo while you mentally sing it, enabling you more easily to locate rhythmically the point of direction change.

Press PLAY

(3)

The performing instrument is *bassoon*.

ANSWER

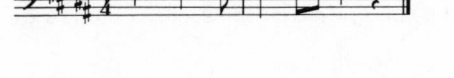

The melody printed above is what you heard the bassoon play. Observe that the change of direction occurred on the accented portion of a beat. No written response required. Proceed to the next frame.

72 Listen to this melody a sufficient number of times to make sure that you can sing it at a slower tempo.

In this frame, the melodic line changes direction on an accented portion of a beat. Indicate the location with an arrow.

Press PLAY

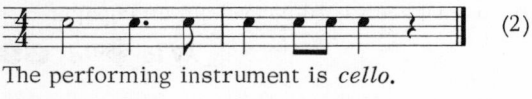

(2)

The performing instrument is *cello*.

ANSWER

The performing instrument is *cello*.

73 Even though you do not have the pitches printed, you can still sing the rhythmic line. Do this before listening to the recorded melody.

After hearing the *violin* play, sing as before. Use your tonal memory to help you locate the point of direction change in the melody.

Press PLAY

(2)

ANSWER

Notice again that the change occurs on an accented portion of a beat—in this case, the second beat of the third measure.

74 The melodic change of direction occurs on the *unaccented* portion of a beat in this *horn* melody.

Press PLAY

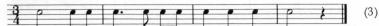 (3)

ANSWER

Tapping the divided beat should be of help in this process. Always sing the melody again before proceeding to the next frame.

---

75 Indicate the location of melodic direction change in this frame. The performing instrument is *clarinet*.

Press PLAY

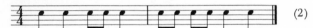 (2)

ANSWER

---

76 This *trombone* melody contains two changes of direction in the melody. Both occur on accented portions of the beats involved. Indicate the location as before.

Press PLAY

 (3)

ANSWER

---

77 This frame also contains two direction changes. One occurs on an accented portion of a beat, and the other on an unaccented portion. The performing instrument is *trumpet*.

Press PLAY

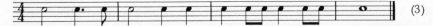 (3)

ANSWER

78 In the next few frames, a portion of the melody will be omitted. Change of direction on notes other than the tonic will be involved. Follow the same procedure of locating the rhythmic point where change occurs *before* attempting to write the omitted notes.

As you well know by this time, locating the rhythmic point of change is made easier when you employ tonal and rhythmic memory. Conduct and tap while you listen and again while you sing the melody to yourself.

Complete the omitted measure.

Press PLAY

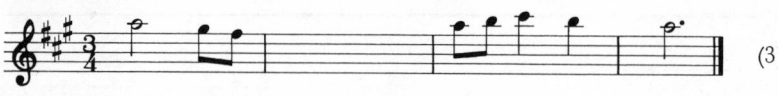

(3)

The performing instrument is *flute*.

ANSWER

Observe that the change of direction occurs on the second beat of the missing measure.

Had change of direction occurred on beat 1 of the second measure:

additional direction change would have been heard in the third measure.

If direction change had not occurred until beat 3 of the second measure:

an interval skip would have been heard.

---

79 This frame omits two measures. The change of direction involved occurs on an unaccented portion of a beat. After you have located the rhythmic point of change, complete the omitted measures.

If your response in this frame contains more than one direction change, or if it contains an interval skip, you have changed direction at the wrong point.

Press PLAY

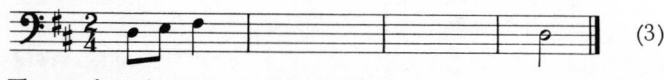

(3)

The performing instrument is *piano*.

ANSWER

Continue to conduct and tap while you sing, both before making your response and again after.

80   The omitted section in this frame contains two changes of direction. Locate the rhythmic points of change before writing the omitted melody.

Press PLAY

 (3)

The performing instrument is *bassoon*.

ANSWER

Prior to the playing of each melody you hear the tonic triad sounded. So far, all melodies have begun and ended on the tonic. This emphasis on the *tonal center* of the melodies has a purpose. The purpose is to help you develop a *sense* of the tonal center. Attempt to feel the tonal center in this melody while you sing it. Notice how the melody goes below the tonic, then above, and finally returns to the tonic.

---

81   There are two melodic direction changes in this frame. One occurs on an unaccented portion of a beat. Be aware of the tonal center while listening. Complete the omitted section.

Press PLAY

 (3)

The performing instrument is *violin*.

ANSWER

If you made an error with direction change, you probably had difficulty ending your response on a B (the tonic).

 Play this frame's melody again, and observe how the next to the last note *leads* to the tonic. (You may have to rewind the tape a short distance to hear the melody again.)

---

82   When you locate the beat where the melodic direction change occurs, determine whether it is on an accented or an unaccented portion of the beat.

 Write the melody you hear played in this frame.

Press PLAY

 (3)

The performing instrument is *trombone*.

ANSWER

In all the following frames, try to maintain the tonal center in your mind's ear while you listen.

83   In the next few frames, the printed melodies will differ from those played. Examine the rhythmic and *tonal* aspects of the printed music before listening. Sing the printed music in order to make it easier to compare what you see with what you will hear.

In this frame the *clarinet* melody will change direction at a rhythmic location different from that indicated in the printed melody. Locate the point of difference and rewrite as before.

Press PLAY

(3)

ANSWER

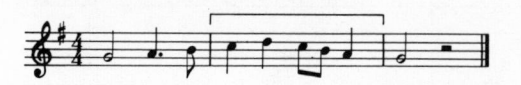

---

84   After making your preliminary examination of the printed music (which will include singing it), listen to the *cello* melody and compare the two. They will differ rhythmically at two places.

Press PLAY

(3)

ANSWER

If you are having difficulty with direction change, it might be well to continue the procedure of marking the rhythmic point of change *before* making your written response.

85   In the preceding two frames, the differences were rhythmic ones. In this frame, the melody will change direction on notes different from those printed. Use the procedure for locating rhythmic point of change.

Press PLAY

(3)

The performing instrument is *horn*.

ANSWER

The value of locating the rhythmic point of change is quite obvious. Had the printed music in the response portion been correct, the point of change would have occurred on an accented portion of a beat. Since the rhythmic point of change was heard on an unaccented portion of a beat, the melody printed here was the only possibility.

---

86   After examining the printed music, compare it with the *trumpet* performance. Locate and correct the difference.

Press PLAY

(2)

ANSWER

---

87 Press PLAY

Another rhythmic device frequently encountered in music is *syncopation*. In syncopation, notes beginning on unaccented parts of the beat are tied over to notes on the accented part of the beat. This produces an effect of shifted location of accent.

   Conduct the metric beat and tap the divided beat while you listen to this syncopated *flute* melody.

(1)

ANSWER

No written response required. Proceed to the next frame.

88 Press PLAY

This frame repeats the pitch outline used in the preceding frame. Conduct while you listen to the melody played without ties.

 (1)

There was no feeling of syncopation in that playing. Listen to the melody again, this time with ties added.

 (1)

The performing instrument is *flute*.

ANSWER

Some persons find it easier to feel the shifted location of accent in syncopation if they are not tapping the divided beat, but are only conducting the metric beat while listening. You might want to experiment with both approaches to determine which works best for you. Proceed to the next frame.

89

In this and the next frame, you will have printed melodies with ties omitted. You will hear a syncopated melody played. Sing the printed music before listening.

After listening to the melodies played once or twice, sing them again, paying particular attention to the places where you had to sing a tied effect not indicated in the printed music.

Add ties which make the printed music correspond to the syncopated *piano* melody you heard and sang.

Press PLAY

 (2)

ANSWER

It is important to conduct the metric beat vigorously in order to accent the location of these beats. By so doing, you will find it easier to locate the shift of the accent in the syncopated sections.

90

Add the ties which make this printed melody correspond to what you hear.

Press PLAY

 (2)

The performing instrument is *bassoon*.

ANSWER

91 After listening to this *violin* melody, sing it before making your response. Complete the omitted measure. It involves syncopation.

Press PLAY

(3)

The syncopated figure could have been written ♪♩♪ and still be correct. The use of ties provides a visual metrical organization of the rhythm, which makes sight reading easier.

---

92 The omitted measure in this frame involves both syncopation and change of melodic direction. Be able to sing it before you write it.

Press PLAY

(3)

The performing instrument is *horn*.

ANSWER

The arrow indicates the point of melodic direction change. Conduct the beat to help you locate the shift in accent.

---

93 The printed music will provide you with the location of the tonic and the number of metric beats for each measure.

Listen for change of melodic direction and syncopation in this melody. Be able to sing it before writing your response. Complete the omitted section.

Press PLAY

(3)

The performing instrument is *cello*.

ANSWER

Observe that the first change of direction occurs on an unaccented portion of a beat. This point corresponds to a shift in the rhythmic accent. If you had difficulty completing this omitted section, it might be helpful to:

1. Conduct the metric beat vigorously.
2. Locate the rhythmic points of melodic change as before.
3. Locate the point where there is a shift of accent.

Do these steps in the order indicated.

After you have checked your response, sing the melody while conducting the beat. After you have done this, proceed to the next frame.

94   This frame involves a rest, in addition to syncopation and change of melodic direction. Locate your probable starting note before you listen. It will be the tonic.

Press PLAY

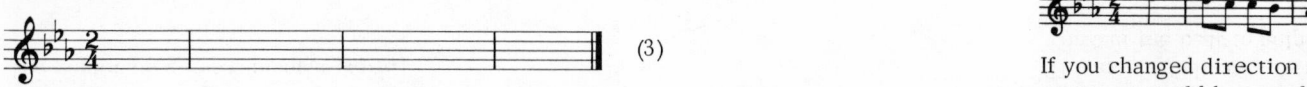

(3)

The performing instrument is *trombone*.

ANSWER

The purpose of the arrow has been to focus your attention on points of melodic change of direction. This will *not* be included in subsequent correct answers in simple meter. It is assumed, though, that you will continue to employ this listening aid in detecting melodic change.

---

95   Locate the tonic before listening. Make sure that your response ends on the tonic. Write this syncopated *clarinet* melody.

Press PLAY

(3)

ANSWER

If you changed direction at the wrong point rhythmically, your response would have ended on a note other than tonic. Notice how the D (seventh degree) *leads* to the E flat (tonic). The seventh degree is called the *leading tone*.

---

96   Write this melody. Listen for rests. If you don't end on the tonic, you have changed direction at the wrong point.

Press PLAY

(3)

The performing instrument is *trumpet*.

ANSWER

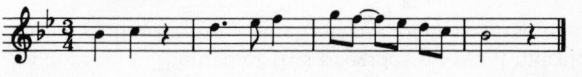

It is to be hoped that your tonal and rhythmic memory has developed to the point where you can accurately sing these syncopated melodies to yourself after only two or three hearings. If you cannot already do so, continue to work toward this end.

97 In the following frames, the printed melody will differ from that which you hear. The difference may be either rhythmic or melodic, or it may be both rhythmic and melodic.

Continue to follow the "prelistening" routine of examining the meter and key signatures, locating the tonic on the staff, and singing the printed melody.

After you have listened to the performing instrument, compare the two melodies. Bracket the location of differences and write on the second staff that which you heard the instrument play at the points of difference.

Press PLAY

(3)

The performing instrument is *piano*.

---

98 Two measures contain differences in this frame. Locate the differences and correct.

Press PLAY

(3)

The performing instrument is *flute*.

Did you observe that measure 2 was a rhythmic repetition of measure 1? Such recognition would make it possible to concentrate your attention on the melodic change of direction.

99 Locate and correct differences in this melody.

Press PLAY

(3)

ANSWER

The performing instrument is *bassoon*.

---

100 Sing this melody several times before listening. The first three measures each contain a point of difference.

Press PLAY

(3)

ANSWER

The performing instrument is *horn*.

---

101 In the preceding frames, various instruments have been heard. After this frame you will be asked to identify these instruments as an additional part of your musical training.

Complete the omitted section of this melody. To prepare yourself for Frame 102, observe also the characteristic low register of the *clarinet*.

Press PLAY

(3)

ANSWER

Observe the repetition of the first part of measure 2 in measure 3. When repetition occurs, use it as an aid in your listening.

Continue to sing the melodies in each frame after you have checked your response.

102   As you heard in the preceding frame, the clarinet can play rather low in pitch. Other instruments can play the same melody at the same pitch, but the *quality of sound* (*timbre* is the technical term) will be different.

Listen to the same melody played twice again. Indicate which time the melody is played by the clarinet.

Press PLAY

The clarinet played the _____ (first, second) time.

ANSWER

The clarinet played the *second* time.

This is the same melody as printed in Frame 101, but in the bass clef to avoid the use of leger lines.

The instrument playing the first time was the bassoon.

---

103   The melody in this frame will be played three times—once each by a different instrument. Indicate which time the melody is played by the clarinet.

After you have done this, sing the melody you heard played by each of the three instruments before writing your response to the two omitted measures.

Press PLAY

The clarinet played the _____ (first, second, third) time.

(3)

ANSWER

The clarinet played the *second* time. The horn played first, the cello third.

Check carefully the accuracy of rests and melodic direction change in your written response before singing this melody again. Conduct and tap while you sing.

104 Not only is the clarinet capable of playing in a low range, but when it does so, you have observed that the sound has a particular and identifying characteristic. Some refer to this sound as "dark."

The *word* used to describe the characteristic sound of an instrument is not as important as the familiarity that results from frequently hearing that instrument. It is this familiarity which permits you to recognize the sound and correctly identify its source.

Compare the different qualities of sound (or timbres) of the *clarinet* as it plays (*a*) its low register and (*b*) its middle register.

Press PLAY

ANSWER

No written response required. Proceed to the next frame.

---

105 In the preceding frame, not only was the second melody higher in pitch, but the quality of sound of the clarinet was different. Complete the omitted section of this melody played by the clarinet in its *middle register*. Be able to sing the melody before writing your response.

Press PLAY

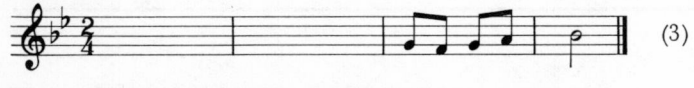

The performing instrument is *clarinet*.

ANSWER

106 The melody in this frame will be played three times—once each by a different instrument. Indicate which time the melody is played by the clarinet. Maintain the tonal center in your thinking while you listen. Complete the omitted measures.

Press PLAY

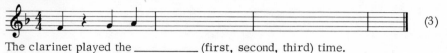

The clarinet played the _____ (first, second, third) time.

The clarinet played the *first* time. The violin played second, the flute third.

---

107 In a frame such as this one, where only the meter signature, the key signature, the clef, and the bar lines are indicated, it is still possible to locate the tonic on the staff (or on leger lines, as is the case here). It is also possible to determine the number of metric beats in a measure.

When you begin to listen to the recorded melody, conduct the metric beat and tap the divided beats. After you have listened a sufficient number of times, sing the melody to yourself.

Let the *leading tone* (seventh degree) aid you in maintaining the tonal center in your thinking.

This frame illustrates still a third characteristic sound of the *clarinet* when it plays in a high register.

Write the melody you hear played.

Press PLAY

When you sing this melody again, observe how the leading tones (marked LT) emphasize the tonal center by "leading" to the D flat (tonic).

108 In a frame such as this one, where there is a melody printed, it is not only possible to determine the information discussed in the preceding frame, but to include a singing of the melody as a part of your examination of the printed music. Be sure to conduct and tap while you sing in order to perceive the printed rhythm.

The melody in this frame will be played three times—once each by a different instrument. Indicate which time the melody is played by the clarinet.

Locate points of difference and rewrite as before. Include clef and key signature in your response.

Press PLAY

(3)

The clarinet played the _____ (first, second, third) time.

---

109 The location of the starting note will be partially determined by identifying the register (low, middle, or high) in which the melody is played. More precision will be brought to the starting note's location by examination of the key signature in order to locate the tonic. (Thus far, all melodies begin and end on the tonic.) Write this short clarinet melody.

Press PLAY

(3)

ANSWER

The clarinet played the *third* time. The piano played first, the flute second.

If you made an error on the second measure, be sure to locate the rhythmic point of melodic direction change as a part of your listening procedure.

Notice that the third measure provides a shift of accent not indicated in the printed music in the response section.

ANSWER

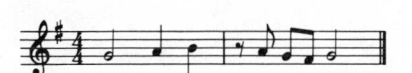

Your response must be considered incorrect if written in the wrong octave. If you find it difficult to discriminate between registers, review Frames 101 to 109, paying particular attention to the differing quality of the clarinet in the three registers.

110 Other instruments have different qualities of sound between their extreme registers, but these differences are not as marked as they are with the clarinet. The low pitches of a wind or string instrument sound "relaxed" or "free" in their quality. On the other hand, the high pitches of an instrument tend to have a "tense" or "strained" quality.

Compare the tone qualities produced when this melody is played in a low range and then in a high range on the bassoon.

Press PLAY

No written response required. Proceed to the next frame.

 (1)

(1)

The performing instrument is *bassoon.*

---

111 It is the difference in quality between the high and low pitches of an instrument that help in discriminating between instruments of similar timbre, such as the trumpet and trombone when playing in the same octave. The melody in this frame is played first by the trumpet in its low register. When played next by the trombone, it will sound in the same octave, but the "more intense" quality of sound produced by the trombone in its upper register will distinguish the performance from the more "relaxed" sound of the trumpet's performance.

Press PLAY

No written response required. Proceed to the next frame.

 (1)

The performing instrument is *trumpet.*

 (1)

The performing instrument is *trombone.*

112   Similarly, the violin and cello can play in the same octave. Like the trumpet and trombone, discrimination is aided by means of the quality of the tone produced, that is, whether it has a "relaxed" or a "tense" quality.

   The melodic fragment in this frame will be played twice—once by a violin and once by a cello. Indicate which time the melody is played by the cello. You can expect it to have a more "intense" sound than that of the violin.

Press PLAY

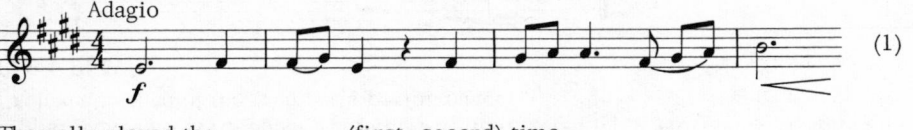

(1)

The cello played the_____(first, second) time.

ANSWER

The cello played the *first* time.

   If you had difficulty detecting a difference of quality in just one hearing, play this frame several times until the difference becomes more apparent.

---

113   Frame 110 illustrated the different qualities of tone in the extreme ranges of the bassoon. In spite of this difference, the bassoon has a characteristic sound throughout its entire range span. This is partly a result of the double reed used to generate the sound.

   Examine the printed music and sing the melody. After you have done this, listen to the bassoon and compare.

   Locate the points of difference in this bassoon melody and write what you hear played at those points.

Press PLAY

(3)

The performing instrument is *bassoon*.

ANSWER

Measure 2 is a pitch difference and measure 4 is a rhythmic one.

114 The horn, though a brass instrument like the trumpet and trombone, has a tone quality all its own. It might be described as being "covered" or "mellow." Again, the words which might describe it are less important than the ability which you develop to recognize it when hearing it played.

Locate and correct the points of difference in this horn melody.

Press PLAY

 (3)

The performing instrument is *horn*.

---

115 The horn and bassoon are two of the instruments in a woodwind quintet. (The horn, though a brass instrument, is included as a standard member of the woodwind quintet.) Indicate whether horn or bassoon is playing this melody. Complete the missing measures.

Press PLAY

 (3)

The performing· instrument is _____.

The performing instrument is *horn*.

Check your answer carefully for rests and syncopation. After you have done this, compare the timbre of the horn with that of the bassoon playing the same melody.

Press PLAY

116 The flute has a clear and somewhat penetrating tone in its upper register and a tone which might be called "breathy" in its lower register. Listen to the *flute* play this melody, first as written, then one octave higher, and finally, two octaves higher.

Press PLAY

ANSWER

No written response required. Proceed to the next frame.

 (1)

 (1)

 (1)

---

117 The melody in this frame will be played three times—once each by a different instrument. Indicate which time the melody is played by the flute.

After you have done this, sing the melody you heard played by each of the three instruments before writing your response to the two omitted measures.

Press PLAY

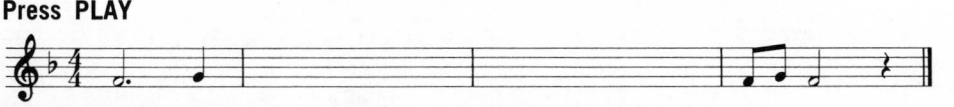 (3)

The flute played the _____ (first, second, third) time.

ANSWER

The flute played the *third* time. The trumpet played first, the violin second.

Before proceeding with the program, complete the test items for Test 2, which will be found at the back of the book. Obtain the tape-recorded materials for this test from your instructor.

118 Press PLAY

Until now, all frames have employed simple meter, that is, beats which divide into two parts. The next frames will introduce *compound meter*, that is, beats which *divide into three parts*.

In the preceding frames the quarter note (♩) was used as the metric beat. In this introduction to *compound meter*, the dotted quarter note (♩.) will be used as the metric beat.

Conduct the metric beats (two beats per measure), which are located by the arrows, while you listen to this rhythmic line in compound meter. After you have done this, complete the statement below.

(1)

Because this rhythmic line's metric beats are grouped in two's, it is called duple meter. Because each beat *divides* into three parts, (see bracketed sections) it is called _____ meter.

The performing instrument is *trombone*.

ANSWER

compound

Your conductor pattern for $\frac{6}{8}$ meter will be a duple pattern, the same as that used for $\frac{2}{4}$ meter. Conductor patterns for the other compound meters used in this program are:

$\frac{9}{8}$ = triple pattern

$\frac{12}{8}$ = quadruple pattern

For information on the conductor beat patterns, refer to the chart on page 215.

119 Press PLAY

This frame contains rhythmic notation which can be grouped into patterns of four metric beats. Listen to this line in quadruple meter, conducting a quadruple beat pattern while you listen.

After you have listened to the line played once, stop the machine and put in the bar lines to make the printed line correspond to the quadruple signature, that is, $\frac{12}{8}$.

Remember that a dotted quarter note ($\downarrow\cdot$) or its equivalent constitutes a metric beat.

(1)

The performing instrument is *cello*.

ANSWER

Your bar lines should have been at the places indicated by the brackets.

If you have made an error in your placement of the bar lines, rewrite the rhythmic line on the second staff, and correctly place the bar lines.

As you listen to this rhythmic line played again, notice particularly how the beats can be felt in groups of four.

After you have listened, sing the rhythmic line as you conduct the beats.

Press PLAY

120 Press PLAY

The difference between simple and compound meter is found in the way each beat is divided.

This line is in simple meter because its beats divide into two parts. Notice how the eighth-note beams bind the eighth notes together in groups of two.

(1)

This line is similar to the preceding one, except that the beats in this line divide into three, making it compound meter. Notice how the eighth-note beams bind the eighth notes into groups of three.

(1)

The performing instrument is *trumpet*.

ANSWER

No written response required. Proceed to the next frame.

121 In this frame, mark an arrow above the notes where each beat begins. Because this rhythmic line is in duple meter, make certain that you have two beats indicated for each measure.

Do not press PLAY until you have checked your response with the correct answer.

The performing instrument is *piano*.

ANSWER

(2)

After checking your answer, correct it if necessary.

This rhythmic line is recorded twice on the tape. Conduct a duple beat pattern along with the first presentation. Sing the rhythmic line along with the second presentation while continuing to conduct the meter.

Press PLAY

---

122 Probably the easiest compound division of the metric beat to recognize aurally is in the pattern of three eighth notes (♪♪♪). As you conduct the metric beat with one hand, tap the three divisions of each beat with the other. Sing what you hear played before writing your response.

Complete the omitted measure in this frame. It will contain a ♪♪♪ pattern.

Press PLAY

(2)

The performing instrument is *violin*.

ANSWER

Observe that the last measure must have ♩. ♩. to complete the three beats since ♩. is equal to one metric beat.

123   In compound meter as used in this program:

♩. = 1 metric beat

𝅗𝅥. = 2 metric beats

In the response, draw a circle around the letters whose note values equal four metric beats in compound meter.

Do not press PLAY

(a)   *(b)*   *(c)*   *(d)*

ANSWER

(b)   *(c)*

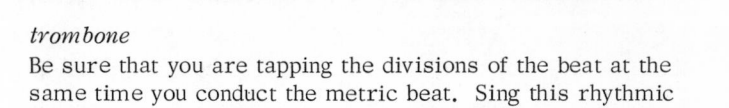

a contains only three beats. *d* contains four beats in simple meter but not in compound meter.

   If you made an error, review frame 120. It will not be necessary to listen to the tape; only review the written instructions.

---

124   Examine the printed music for this frame. After listening to the recorded rhythmic line, sing it to yourself several times before writing your response. Indicate the instrument playing and complete the omitted section.

Press PLAY

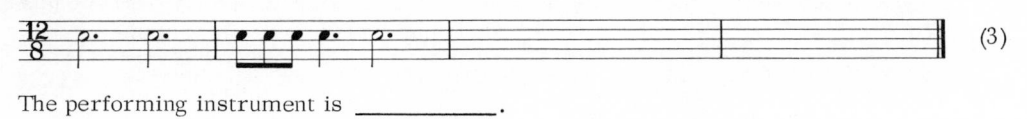

(3)

The performing instrument is _____ .

ANSWER

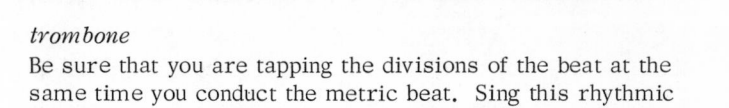

trombone

Be sure that you are tapping the divisions of the beat at the same time you conduct the metric beat. Sing this rhythmic line again before proceeding to the next frame.

125 Thus far, the following rhythmic units of one metric beat or more have been used in compound meter:

- 𝅝· which gets four beats
- 𝅗𝅥· 𝅗𝅥· which gets three beats
- 𝅗𝅥· which gets two beats
- ♩· which gets one beat

In addition to these, the rhythmic pattern , formed by the compound division of one beat, has been used.

♩ ♪ is another rhythmic pattern frequently used in compound meter. Conduct and tap while you listen.

Press PLAY

$\frac{6}{8}$ (1)

The performing instrument is _____.

ANSWER

cello

---

126 The rhythmic pattern ♩ ♪ in compound meter occurs within the duration of one metric beat (♩·) and is the equivalent of tying the first two subdivisions of the beat ().

Conduct and tap while listening to these two rhythmic lines played. Observe that both lines are alike in sound.

Press PLAY

$\frac{9}{8}$ (1)

$\frac{9}{8}$ (1)

The performing instrument is _____.

ANSWER

piano
Notice that a combination of rests (𝄾 𝄿) is necessary in the last measure to constitute one metric beat.

127 The procedure of tapping the divided beats and conducting the metric beats while listening to the recorded examples is an important one. Equally important is being able to sing to yourself the melody which you hear played. It is desirable to be able to do this after three or *less* hearings.

The omitted section in this frame has the rhythmic pattern ♩ ♪ on one of its beats.

Press PLAY

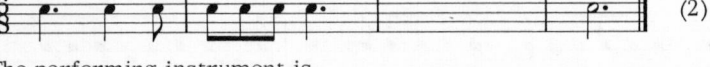

(2)

The performing instrument is _____.

ANSWER

trumpet

In addition to the cue that your response should contain ♩ ♪, you also had the assistance of repetition of the first measure.

---

128 For crisp, staccato passages, the rhythmic figure ♩ ♪ is sometimes written ♩ 𝄽 ♩ . The general feeling of the rhythmic pattern remains the same but a difference no less exists.

Notice the similarity at the same time you observe the difference between the two bracketed sections in this rhythmic line.

Press PLAY

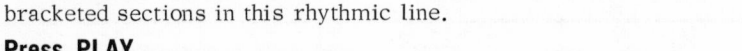

(1)

The performing instrument is _____.

ANSWER

flute

Because the general feeling of ♩ ♪ and ♩ 𝄽 ♩ is so similar, there will be times when it becomes difficult to discriminate between the two. For the time being, do not consider it an error of response if you should write one when the other has been played. Always attempt to make the discrimination, however. Later in this program you will be expected to make this discrimination.

---

129 The omitted measures in the following frames can be completed with rhythmic patterns selected from:

Conduct and tap while you listen. Sing the rhythmic line before making your response.

Press PLAY

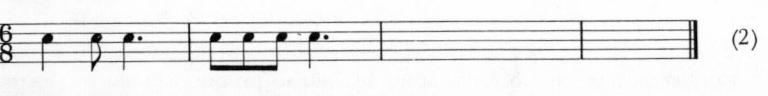

(2)

The performing instrument is _____.

ANSWER

bassoon

130 Complete the omitted measures. They will involve three of the patterns outlined in Frame 129, as well as rests.

Press PLAY

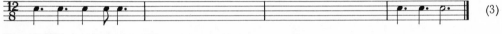

The performing instrument is _____.

(3)

trombone

If you used ♩♪ in measure 3, listen again and observe that the trombone does not sustain the first eighth note of the pattern through the rest. Your response must have contained the rests in the final measure. They should be in the order indicated.

---

131 Complete the omitted measures.

Press PLAY

The performing instrument is _____.

(3)

piano

---

132 In the next few frames, the printed rhythmic patterns on certain metric beats will differ from that which you hear. Locate the points of rhythmic difference with a bracket and write the pattern you hear on the second staff. All corrections can be made with one or more of the following:

$$\quad \text{♩.} \quad \text{♩.} \quad \text{♫♫} \quad \text{♩ ♪} \quad \text{♪♪}$$

This frame contains only one point of difference.

Press PLAY

The performing instrument is _____.

(2)

horn

It is hoped that by this time your response was not ♩♪.

133 This frame contains one point of difference.

Press PLAY

(2)

clarinet

The performing instrument is _____.

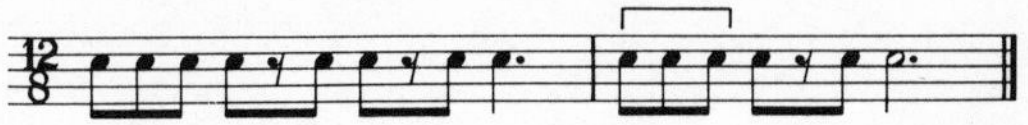

---

134 This frame contains two points of difference.

Press PLAY

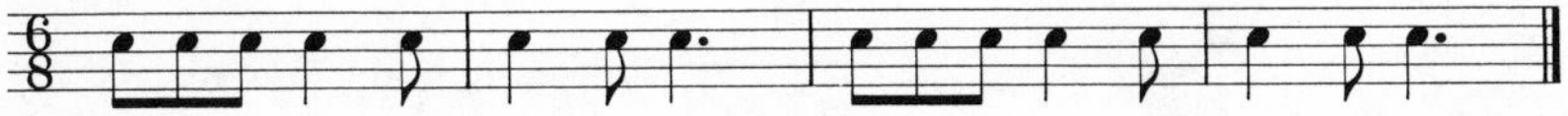

(2)

ANSWER

violin

The performing instrument is _____.

---

135 In this frame, rhythmic differences are found in three successive metric beats.

Press PLAY

(3)

ANSWER

cello

The performing instrument is _____.

136   The melodies in this and the next frame will be rhythmic adaptations in compound meter of major scales. Apply these instructions to each:

1. Locate the metric beats with arrows (see Frame 9).
2. Conduct the metric beat and tap the three compound subdivisions.
3. Sing the melody while doing step 2 above.
4. Press PLAY and listen to the melody.
5. Check your response with the correct answer.

After you have done steps 1, 2, and 3, press PLAY.

(1)

The performing instrument is _____ .

ANSWER

trumpet
Be sure that instrument identification was part of your response.

---

137   Follow the procedure outlined in Frame 136. After you have done steps 1, 2, and 3, press PLAY.

(1)

The performing instrument is _____ .

ANSWER

piano

---

138   This frame and the next provide only the rhythmic notation of the melodies played. You are to place an arrow over the note in the rhythmic notation where you hear the change of melodic direction occur (see Frame 71).

Conduct and tap while you listen. After listening to the melody once or twice, sing it precisely as you heard it. If you can do this, you will be able to slow the tempo while you mentally sing it, enabling you more easily to locate rhythmically the point of direction change.

In this frame, the melodic line changes direction on an accented portion of a beat.

Press PLAY

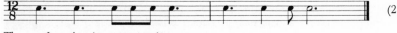

(2)

The performing instrument is _____ .

ANSWER

bassoon

139 This melody changes direction in two places. Both are on accented portions of the beat. Indicate the location of change with arrows as before.

Press PLAY

(2)

The performing instrument is _____ .

ANSWER

piano

---

140 In the following frames, a portion of the printed melody will be omitted. Supply the missing note or notes with one of these compound rhythmic patterns:

Press PLAY

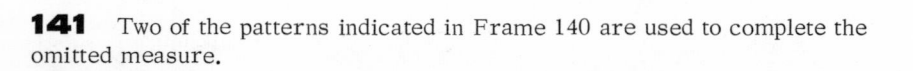

(2)

The performing instrument is _____ .

ANSWER

trombone
Observe that the change of direction occurred on the accented portion of the beat.

---

141 Two of the patterns indicated in Frame 140 are used to complete the omitted measure.

Press PLAY

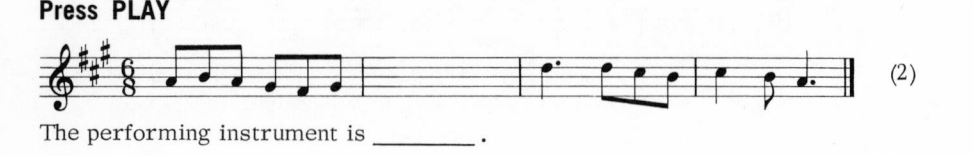

(2)

The performing instrument is _____ .

ANSWER

flute
You may have written the first beat of measure 2 with the pattern ♩ 𝄾 ♩. You should begin now to be more discriminating between these two similar patterns. If you made this error, listen to this frame again and notice how the flute sustains the quarter note for its full value.

142   Complete the omitted measure.

Press PLAY

(2)

The performing instrument is _____.

ANSWER

trumpet

---

143   Complete the omitted measure.

Press PLAY

(2)

The performing instrument is _____.

ANSWER

violin

---

144   Carefully examine the meter and key signatures before listening to this frame. Observe that this melody does not begin on the tonic as all preceding melodies have done. More will be said about this in Frame 167.

   Complete the omitted section of this melody.

Press PLAY

(3)

The performing instrument is _____.

ANSWER

horn

Here is another good illustration of the leading tone positively identifying the last note as tonic.

145 When you listen, observe that there is a melodic direction change on the second beat of the omitted measure. It is on an accented portion of the beat.

Complete the omitted measure.

Press PLAY

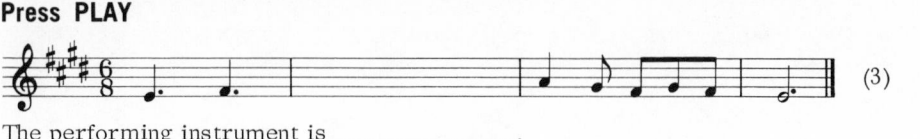

(3)

The performing instrument is _____.

ANSWER

horn

If it will be helpful, continue to locate the rhythmic points of melodic direction change with an arrow before writing. If you do not do so on paper, at least do so in your thinking. Sing this melody again before proceeding to the next frame.

---

146 The omitted measure has a melodic direction change on an accented portion of a beat. Locate the point of change before writing your response.

Press PLAY

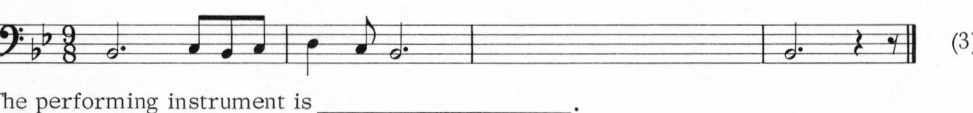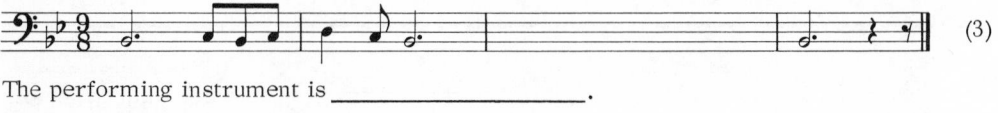

(3)

The performing instrument is _____.

ANSWER

bassoon

---

147 Locate the tonic before you listen. Your response must contain two direction changes. Both will occur on accented portions of the beats in which they appear.

Press PLAY

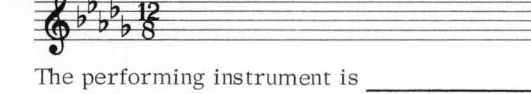

(3)

The performing instrument is _____.

ANSWER

trumpet

148 Complete the omitted measures.

Press PLAY

The performing instrument is _____ .

(3)

ANSWER

cello

---

149 Listen for a rest in this melody. Remember that a one-beat rest in compound meter is indicated with a combination of two rests.

Complete the omitted measures.

Press PLAY

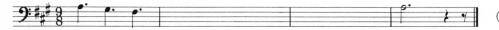

The performing instrument is _____ .

(3)

ANSWER

trombone

---

150 **Press PLAY**

Change of melodic direction may occur on the third portion of the compound division of the metric beat. When it does, it is in one of two ways: (1) the second note of a two-note pattern, for example, ♪ ♪ , or (2) the third note of a three-note pattern, for example, ♪♪♪ .

Listen to this short melody in which there is direction change on the last note of the ♪ ♪ pattern.

(2)

Listen again and observe how the extreme notes can be heard as the final note in a line with the direction change occurring as a *pick-up beat* (*anacrusis* is the technical term) to the next line. The performing instrument is _____ .

ANSWER

cello

151 Place an arrow over the note in the rhythmic notation where you hear the change of melodic direction occur.

In this frame, the melodic line changes direction on a ♪ ♪ pattern. Be able to sing the melody to yourself before writing your response.

Press PLAY

The performing instrument is _____ .

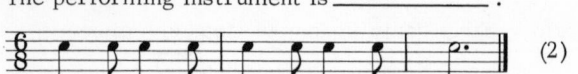

(2)

flute

---

152 Indicate the rhythmic location of direction change in this melody.

Press PLAY

(2)

The performing instrument is _____ .

trombone

---

153 This melody changes direction in two places. Both are on the last note of the two-note pattern, ♪ ♪. Indicate the location of change with arrows as before.

Press PLAY

(3)

The performing instrument is _____ .

violin

154 The melodic direction change in this omitted measure occurs on a  pattern. Locate the point of change before writing your response. Locating that point will be made easier if you can sing the melody to yourself at a slower tempo.

Press PLAY

(2)

The performing instrument is_____ .

ANSWER

piano

---

155 Locate the rhythmic points of direction change before writing your response.

Press PLAY

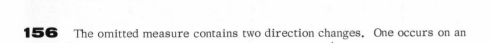

(3)

The performing instrument is_____ .

ANSWER

clarinet

---

156 The omitted measure contains two direction changes. One occurs on an accented portion of a beat. The other occurs in the  pattern.

Examine the meter and key signatures before listening. Locate the tonic on the staff.

After you have listened to the recording, sing the melody to yourself and locate the rhythmic points of melodic direction change.

Complete the omitted section.

Press PLAY

(3)

The performing instrument is_____ .

ANSWER

bassoon

157 Conduct and tap while you listen. The omitted measure involves direction change.

Press PLAY

The performing instrument is _____ .

(3)

ANSWER

horn
Sing this melody again after checking your response.

---

158 Use direction change as well as rests in your response. Listen particularly for the duration of notes.

Press PLAY

The performing instrument is _____ .

(3)

ANSWER

trumpet

---

159 Press PLAY

The preceding frames have dealt with change of melodic direction on the two-note

pattern, 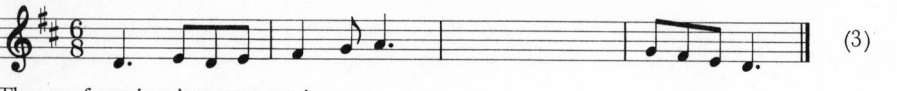. Change on the third portion of the compound metric beat also occurs

on the three-note pattern, . When this is found in stepwise motion, the

second note is heard as a neighboring tone to the two notes on either side of it.

Observe the bracketed sections while you listen to this example.

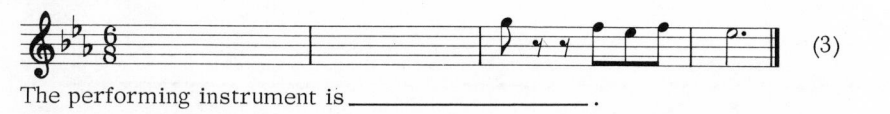

Db ⟶ C   G ⟶ Ab

(1)

In this pattern observe the strong rhythmic feeling of D flat to C and of G to A flat. The performing instrument is _____ .

ANSWER

flute

160   Place an arrow over the note in the rhythmic notation where you hear the change of melodic direction occur. In this frame, the melodic line changes direction on a  pattern. Listen for the neighboring-tone effect on beat 1 of the second measure. Listen for the scalewise progression of C on beat 1 moving to B flat on beat 2 in the second measure. Sing the melody before making your response.

Press PLAY

(2)

The performing instrument is_____ .

ANSWER

violin

---

161   This melody contains two points of melodic direction change. Both involve the pattern. Indicate the points of change with arrows as before.

Press PLAY

(3)

The performing instrument is_____ .

ANSWER

cello

---

162   Locate the point of change before writing your response.

Press PLAY

(3)

The performing instrument is _____ .

ANSWER

piano

If the final note in your response was rhythmically shorter than that indicated in the correct answer, do not consider it incorrect. Due to the rapid fading away of tone after a key has been struck on a piano, it is difficult to perceive precisely the duration of a tone which is held for a considerable length of time.

163 Your written response to the frames in this program must ultimately be to the recorded melodies. As you have discovered by this time, much can be done before you actually listen to the tapes.

Before listening to the melody in this frame, you should determine the tonic and establish in your mind its locations on the staff. Being able to sing the melody after hearing it played will help you locate the rhythmic point of direction change.

Press PLAY

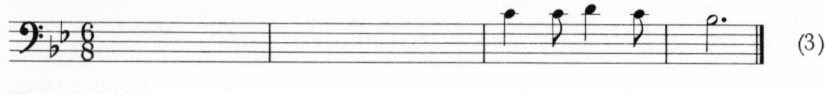

(3)

The performing instrument is _____.

ANSWER

trombone

In spite of the fact that there are three notes in the first metric beat of the second measure, observe how the entire metric beat can be heard as an E flat moving down to the D of the second beat of that measure. This is due to the fact that the F in that first beat is heard as a neighboring-tone effect. If you have listened to all presentations of this melody, rewind the tape a short distance and listen to the melody once more for the effect described above.

---

164 This omitted measure contains three direction changes, the first of which is on the first note. Determine the rhythmic location of the other two before writing your response. Complete the omitted measure.

Press PLAY

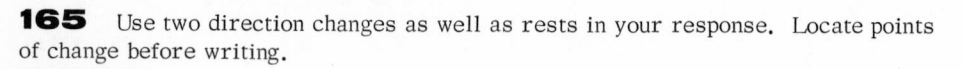

(3)

The performing instrument is _____.

ANSWER

piano

---

165 Use two direction changes as well as rests in your response. Locate points of change before writing.

Press PLAY

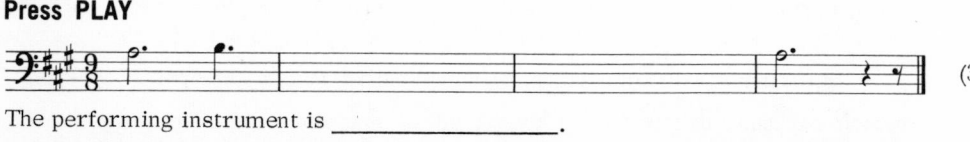

(3)

The performing instrument is _____.

ANSWER

bassoon

Sing this melody again after having checked your response.

166 Complete the missing section.

Press PLAY

(3)

The performing instrument is _____ .

horn

TEST 3

Before proceeding with the program, complete the test items for Test 3, which will be found at the back of the book. Obtain the tape-recorded materials for this test from your instructor.

167 **Press PLAY**

In all previous frames, melodies involving a response to the first note have begun on the tonic. Obviously composers do not limit themselves to such a restriction.

It is appropriate now to learn how to determine the starting note when it is other than the tonic. Listen to this melody, which begins on the third degree of the scale.

(1)

The performing instrument is _____ .

ANSWER

flute

168   In preceding frames, you were instructed to follow several "prelistening" procedures. One of these was to examine the key signature and locate the places where the tonic could appear on the staff in that particular major key. This routine was quite adequate for melodies that would begin on the tonic.

All melodies do not begin on the tonic, but most will begin on a note found in the tonic triad. As you perhaps know, the tonic triad consists of the first, third, and fifth degrees of the scale. (The tonic is the first degree of the scale.) Listen to the piano play this tonic triad in the key of C major.

Press PLAY

ANSWER

No written response required. Proceed to the next frame.

---

169   When you examine the music before listening to the recorded melodies, mentally catalog the different places where the *tonic*, the *third* degree, and the *fifth* degree could be located on the staff, as in this example.

Do not press PLAY

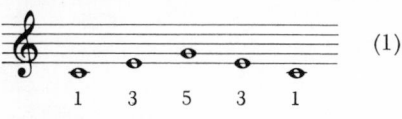

ANSWER

No written response required. Proceed to the next frame.

---

170   Since nearly all melodies begin on a note found in the tonic triad, when you mentally locate the notes of the tonic triad on the staff, you form a catalog of possible starting notes for the melody which follows.

This procedure should *always* precede the listening to the recorded melodies.

In this frame you are given a key signature. Write in the locations of the tonic, the third, and the fifth on the staff.

Do not press PLAY

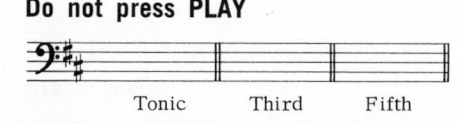

ANSWER

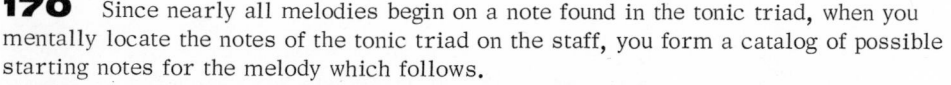

Your response should have included at least one octave of the notes, as in the fifth. It might be well to include notes which lie on, or just beyond, the second leger line, because occasionally melodies will begin at these extremes.

171 Write the locations on the staff of the tonic, third, and fifth for this major key.

Do not press PLAY

Tonic   Third   Fifth

Tonic   Third   Fifth

---

172 Press PLAY

After you have mentally located the places where the tonic, third, and fifth degrees can appear on the staff, you are ready to match these locations with their sounds.

In preceding frames, you have obtained the tonality or key feeling by hearing an outline of the tonic triad played.

From now on, make a habit of *mentally singing* these degrees while they are being sounded. Mentally (that is, *silently*) sing the numbers or syllables while this tonic triad is being played. The performing instrument is *cello*.

No written response required. Proceed to the next frame.

Instrument plays:

(1)

Mentally sing:

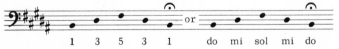

1   3   5   3   1   do   mi   sol   mi   do

173 Press PLAY

In the next four frames, an instrument will play the beginning notes of a melody which will begin on the tonic, the third, or the fifth degree of the scale, as in this example. Each melody will be introduced with the tonic triad as preceding melodies have been. You are to:

1. Examine the key signature and write the locations of the tonic, third, and fifth degrees as you did in Frames 170 and 171.
2. Mentally sing the outline of the tonic triad while the instrument plays it.
3. Write down the first note of the melody played and the instrument performing it.

D Flat Major:

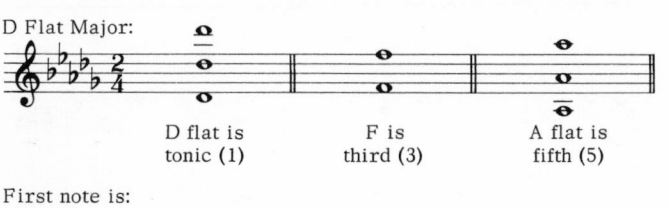

D flat is tonic (1)   F is third (3)   A flat is fifth (5)

First note is:

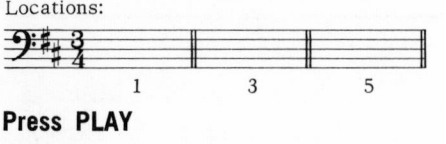

(1)

(3, mi)

The performing instrument is _____.

ANSWER

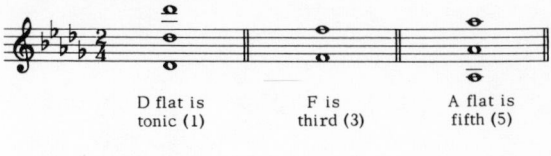

D flat is tonic (1)   F is third (3)   A flat is fifth (5)

3, mi

trumpet

Your response to the played portion of the frame need only contain the first note played and the name of the performing instrument.

174

On the first staff, write the locations of 1, 3 and 5. Do this now before listening to the recorded melody. Mentally sing the tonic triad while you listen and match these sounds with your notation on the first staff. Write the first note of the melody on the second staff.

Locations:

1   3   5

Press PLAY

First note:

(2)

The performing instrument is _____.

ANSWER

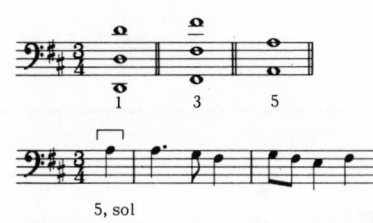

1   3   5

5, sol

trombone

When determining the starting note, it will be helpful to write down the number name or syllable name of the note as you match the sound with your written locations of 1, 3, and 5. This can then be translated to the written note itself.

175   It is not enough to determine that the starting note is the third degree, the fifth degree, or the tonic. It is also necessary to determine the octave. This will be accomplished by (1) determining the performing instrument and (2) determining whether the melody is being played in the low, middle, or upper register of the instrument.

Follow the same procedure in this frame as in the preceding one.

Locations:

Press PLAY

First note:

   (2)

The performing instrument is _____.

ANSWER

flute

---

176   Always orient yourself as much as possible to the problems in each frame *before* the problems actually begin. Do not wait until you are hearing the melody played to examine the rhythm and pitch aspects which are already indicated in the printed music. Take care of these prior to listening.

Follow the same procedure in this frame as in the preceding one. Press PLAY after you have written the locations of 1, 3, and 5.

Locations:

First note:

   (2)

The performing instrument is _____.

ANSWER

violin

177   Follow the same procedure again in this frame. Press PLAY after you have written the locations of 1, 3, and 5.

Locations:

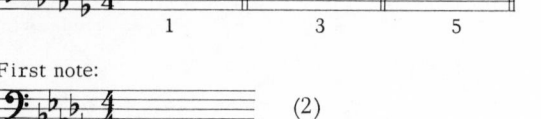

First note:

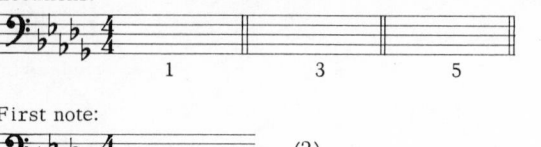   (2)

The performing instrument is _____ .

ANSWER

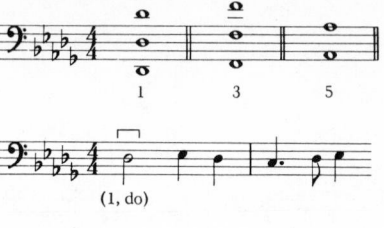

(1, do)

bassoon

---

178   In the following frames, the melodies will begin on notes other than the tonic.

Instead of writing the locations of 1, 3, and 5 on the staff, write in the letter names of the notes for these degrees of the scale in the blanks provided. Do this *before* you listen to the melodies played. Examine the meter signature and the rhythmic aspects of the printed music before you listen. Complete the missing section and indicate the performing instrument.

Press PLAY

1. _____   3. _____   5. _____

   (3)

The performing instrument is _____ .

ANSWER

1. F   3. A   5. C

(3, mi)

piano

It is assumed that you are singing each of these frames' melodies, once before writing your response and again after you have checked the correct answer. Continue to conduct the metric beat and tap the divisions of the beat while listening to the recordings, as well as while singing the melodies.

Your listening technique might be improved by:

1. During and after the first playing:
   a. Determine the first note of the melody.
   b. Determine rhythmic patterns in the omitted section.
   c. Attempt to sing to yourself what was played.
2. During and after the second playing:
   a. Observe where your sung version differed from what was played.
   b. Determine the direction of the melodic line.
   c. Determine rhythmic points of direction change.
   d. Complete your written response.
3. The third playing can be used to check your response.

179   After you have accomplished all that can be done *prior to listening* by examining the printed music, you are prepared to listen more effectively. Follow the listening technique described in the preceding frame while you listen to this melody.

Press PLAY

1. _____   3. _____   5. _____

(3)

The performing instrument is _____ .

ANSWER

1. D   3. F sharp   5. A

(5, sol)

horn

You may find that the order of procedure suggested in the preceding frame does not work for you. Experiment with different orders of these processes until you find one that permits you to make your most effective responses.

   If you are having difficulty locating the starting note, review Frames 168 to 178 before proceeding to the next frame.

---

180   After you have written the names of the notes which comprise 1, 3, and 5 and have followed the other "prelistening" procedures, listen to this melody. Follow the steps for listening suggested in Frame 178 or any modification of them that works better for you.

Press PLAY

1. _____   3. ____   5. ____

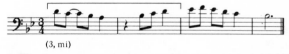

(3)

The performing instrument is _____ .

ANSWER

1. B flat   3. D   5. F

(3, mi)

cello

Be aware of the tonal center while you listen. Observe how the last note of the first measure serves to identify B flat as the tonal center. It does this because it is the *leading tone*.

181 Tapping the compound divisions of the beat will help you determine the rhythm of the second measure in this frame. No rests are needed in your response. Indicate the tonic triad notes before listening. Use the listening procedure suggested in Frame 178 while listening to this melody.

Press PLAY

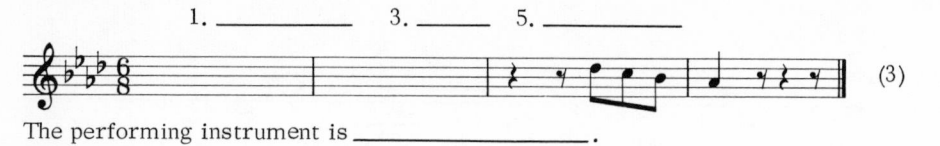

The performing instrument is _____.

ANSWER

1. A flat   3. C   5. E flat

(5, sol)

trumpet

---

182 This frame contains a short two-measure melody beginning on either the third or the fifth degree of the scale. Use the listening routine outlined in Frame 178.

Press PLAY

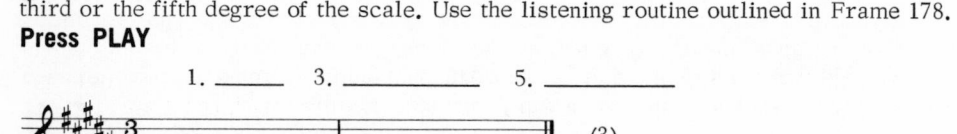

The performing instrument is _____.

ANSWER

1. B   3. D sharp   5. F sharp

flute

The key signature identified this as a melody in B major. The leading tone next to the final note provided the audible identity of B major.

Sing this melody again, but omit the final note. Observe how you are "led" to sing the final note (B). Use this phenomenon of sound (it is called the leading-tone function) whenever possible to help you accurately notate what you hear played.

183 You will no longer be required to write a response indicating the names of the notes in the tonic triad or the notes themselves, as you were in the preceding nine frames. However, it is important that you continue to do this mentally if not on paper. After you have heard the melody played, sing it before making your written response. Listen for a rest in this short melody.

Press PLAY

 (3)

The performing instrument is _____ .

ANSWER

bassoon

After you have checked your response, follow the printed music carefully while singing it again. Notice how the tonal center is established in the first measure by the leading tone.

---

184 Write this melody.

Press PLAY

 (3)

The performing instrument is _____ .

ANSWER

piano

---

185 This frame contains a short two-measure melody beginning on a note other than the tonic. Determine which and write the melody. Follow the listening procedure outlined in Frame 178.

Press PLAY

(3)

The performing instrument is _____ .

ANSWER

trombone

Be sure that your response contained the rests indicated. If it did not, listen to this melodic line again. After you have done this, sing the correct response before proceeding to the next frame.

186 Determine the notes of the tonic triad before listening. Write this short melody. Listen for a rest.

Press PLAY

(3)

The performing instrument is _____.

ANSWER

violin

---

187 The remaining melodies in major keys will begin on the tonic, the third, or the fifth degrees of the scale.

In the next few frames, the printed melody will differ from that which you hear. The difference will be either rhythmic or melodic, or it will be both rhythmic and melodic. Examine all aspects of the printed music, including singing it before listening to it played. Prepare for starting notes other than the tonic. Bracket and correct points of difference. In this frame, the difference will be melodic.

Press PLAY

(3)

The performing instrument is _____.

ANSWER

horn
Sing the line now as you heard it played.

188 Examination of the printed music before listening should include:

1. Locating the metric beats in the melody
2. An awareness of rhythmic devices used in the melody, such as dotted rhythm, divided beats, rests, and syncopation
3. A knowledge of the key, including the location on the staff (and the names) of the notes in the tonic triad
4. A singing of the printed melody, using the correct rhythm indicated

After you have done these "prelistening" steps, locate a melodic difference and a rhythmic difference in this frame.

Press PLAY

(3)

The performing instrument is_____.

cello

Observe that the melodic difference extends over the bar line. Sing the corrected melody played by the cello.

---

189 There is only one point of difference in this melody, but it involves both melody and rhythm.

Press PLAY

(3)

The performing instrument is_____.

trombone

If you mentally cataloged the notes of the tonic before and during the time they were being played, you probably had no difficulty determining the starting note. If you did have difficulty with this, review Frames 168 to 178 before proceeding to the next frame.

190   There are two points of difference in this melody.

Press PLAY

(3)

The performing instrument is_____ .

ANSWER

violin

If the starting note was not obvious to you, notice that the violin melody had a direction change at the beginning of the second measure. The rhythmic repetition in measures 1 and 3 serves as a cue for detecting the second difference in this frame. Make use of all possible cues in your listening.

---

191   This frame contains more than one point of difference. Sing the printed melody before listening to the recorded version.

Press PLAY

(3)

The performing instrument is_____ .

ANSWER

trumpet

192   Until this time, only the following notes and their corresponding rests have been used in the melodies:

With the use of sixteenth notes (♪) several additional rhythmic possibilities are provided.

   Listen to this melody containing sixteenth notes. Conduct the metric beat and tap the eighth-note subdivision while you listen.

Press PLAY

The performing instrument is _____.

ANSWER

clarinet

The tempo of a melody may be such that it is possible to tap the sixteenth-note subdivision. When this is the case, it is advisable to do so. If the tempo is too fast to permit tapping, it is important that you think or feel the sixteenth-note pulse within the metric beat.

---

193   This frame presents four rhythmic patterns which use sixteenth notes. Each of these patterns has frequent use in music written in simple meter.

   Conduct the metric beat and tap the sixteenth-note divisions of the beat while you listen to the horn play each example.

   Observe that the patterns on the second staff indicate the sixteenth-note pulses and their locations in the particular pattern being illustrated.

Press PLAY

(1)

(1)

ANSWER

No written response required. Proceed to the next frame.

194 As a rule, students do not appear to have much difficulty recognizing the  pattern when it is played. The pattern is also quite distinguishable. The rhythmic line in this frame contains both these patterns. The line will be played twice.

Conduct the metric beat and tap the sixteenth-note divisions on both playings. Sing the rhythmic line on the second playing.

Press PLAY

(2)

The performing instrument is *trumpet*.

ANSWER

Do not tap the printed rhythm. Tap the four sixteenth-note divisions for each beat.

Proceed to the next frame.

---

195 Complete the omitted section with one of the following patterns:

Press PLAY

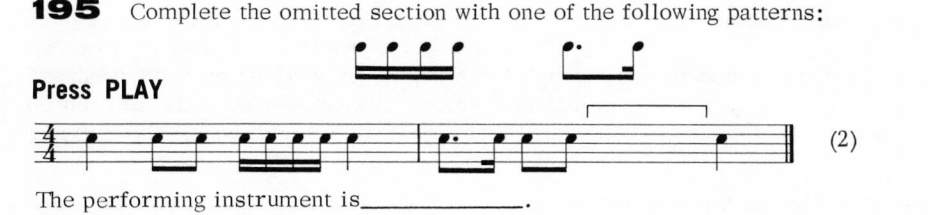

(2)

The performing instrument is_____.

ANSWER

flute

---

196 Both patterns described in the previous frame are used to complete the omitted measure. After hearing the line played, sing it before writing your response.

Press PLAY

(2)

The performing instrument is_____.

ANSWER

trombone

197 A workable technique for distinguishing between  and  is to:

1. Locate the two sixteenth notes played.
2. Determine if they occur on an accented or an unaccented portion of the beat. Compare the sound of the two rhythmic lines in this frame. In the first, the two sixteenth notes are on an accented portion of the beats. In the second, they are on an unaccented portion.

Conduct and tap while you listen. Sing the rhythm along with the second playing of each line.

Press PLAY

The performing instrument is *bassoon*.

No written response required. Proceed to the next frame.

---

198 The omitted section in this frame can be completed with one of the following patterns:

Determine whether the two sixteenth notes in the pattern you hear are on the accented or the unaccented portion of the beat. Singing what you hear will permit you to slow the tempo down sufficiently to make this discrimination easier.

Press PLAY

(2)

The performing instrument is _____ .

piano

199 Both patterns described in the previous frame are used to complete the omitted sections (a different one for each).

Press PLAY

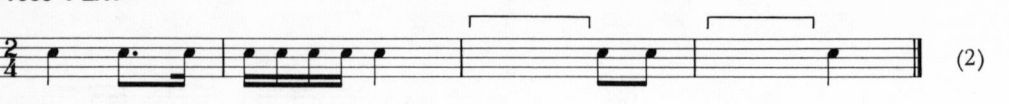

(2)

The performing instrument is_____.

ANSWER

cello

---

200 Complete the omitted section with two of the following rhythmic patterns:

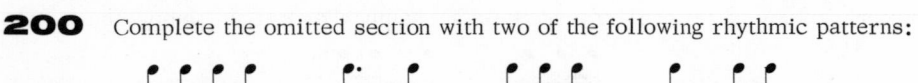

Press PLAY

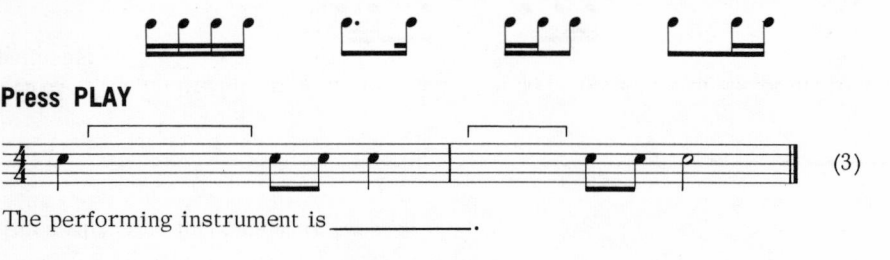

(3)

The performing instrument is_____.

ANSWER

violin
Sing this rhythmic line again, but at a slower tempo in order to feel the location of the two sixteenth notes in measure 2 on an unaccented portion of the beat.

---

201 Complete the omitted portions with two of the patterns outlined in the previous frame.

Press PLAY

(3)

The performing instrument is_____.

ANSWER

horn
After checking your response, *always* sing the melody or rhythmic line played by the performing instrument. Conduct and tap while doing so. Do this even on error-detection frames in which you also sing the melody prior to listening to the performing instrument play it.

202   Your response to this frame will involve sixteenth-note patterns and also previously studied simple-meter patterns.

Press PLAY

The performing instrument is_____.

(3)

---

203 Complete the omitted measure.

Press PLAY

The performing instrument is _____.

(3)

---

204   Complete the missing measures. Sing the rhythmic line you hear before writing your response.

Press PLAY

The performing instrument is_____.

(3)

205 In the following frames, the printed melody will differ from that which you hear. Bracket the location of the difference.

On the second staff, write what you hear played for the bracketed section. The difference will be a rhythmic one and can be written with one or more of the following rhythmic patterns:

As a part of your examination of the printed music, sing the printed melodies in these frames before listening to them played.
Press PLAY after you have sung the melody.

(3)

The performing instrument is_____.

ANSWER

violin

If you had difficulty with this frame, concentrate on the rhythmic location of the two sixteenth notes. Observe that at the point of difference the two sixteenth notes played by the violin were located on an unaccented portion of the beat. Sing this melody while conducting and tapping before proceeding to the next frame.

---

206 In this frame there are two points of rhythmic difference in one measure. Follow the procedure outlined in the preceding frame.

Press PLAY

(3)

The performing instrument is_____.

ANSWER

flute

207 Locate and correct the points of difference in this melody.
Press PLAY after you have sung the melody.

ANSWER

trombone

(3)

The performing instrument is _____ .

---

208 Your response to the omitted measure must contain one of the following rhythmic patterns:

Press PLAY

(3)

The performing instrument is _____ .

ANSWER

cello

209 One of the metric beats in this frame's melody contains a pattern described in the preceding frame. The first note is other than the tonic. Complete the missing measures.

Press PLAY

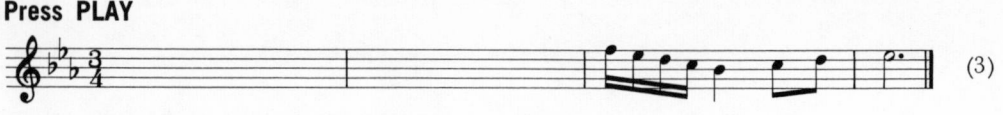

(3)

The performing instrument is_____.

ANSWER

(3, mi)

piano

If you are still having difficulty with the starting note, go over Frames 168 to 178 with your instructor. Your answer did not have to contain the number or syllable (3, mi) if you started

on the correct note. If you had difficulty with the ♪♫ pattern in measure 2, review Frame 197. If you had difficulty with melodic direction change, use arrows to locate rhythmic point of change before writing your response.

---

210 Press PLAY

Melodic direction change can occur within the sixteenth-note patterns being studied. The procedure for locating the rhythmic point of change with the preceding rhythmic patterns is equally valid for sixteenth notes.

Conduct and tap while listening to this melody. It changes melodic direction on a sixteenth note pattern. Sing along with the second playing.

(2)

The performing instrument is_____.

ANSWER

clarinet

211   In addition to the ♩♩♩♩ pattern, it is obvious that the following patterns might also be involved in melodic direction change which takes place on an *accented portion* of a beat:

Place an arrow over the note in the rhythmic notation where you hear a change of melodic direction occur. It will be on an *accented portion* of a beat.

Press PLAY

(2)

The performing instrument is _____ .

horn

---

212   Sing this rhythmic line to yourself before you listen to the recording. After you have done this, listen to the recording and:
1. Sing the melody as you heard it played.
2. Indicate the location of melodic direction change as you did in the preceding frame.

Press PLAY after you have sung this line.

(2)

The performing instrument is _____ .

trombone

Observe that the change occurred on an accented portion of a beat. Sing the melodic line before proceeding to the next frame, even though you sang it prior to your response.

213 In Frame 70, it was said that in simple meter the rhythmic point of direction change could occur on either the accented or the unaccented portion of the beat.

In the sixteenth-note pattern, , the third and fourth notes correspond to the unaccented part of the eighth-note division of the metric beat:

Conduct and tap while listening to this melody. It changes melodic direction in two places, the second of which is on an unaccented portion of a beat. Sing along with the second playing.

Press PLAY

(2)

The performing instrument is_____.

ANSWER

violin

---

214 In addition to the  pattern, melodic direction change on the *unaccented portion* of the beat may also take place in these patterns:

Place an arrow over the note in the rhythmic notation where you hear a change of melodic direction occur. It will be on an unaccented portion of a beat. Sing the melodic line before writing your response.

Press PLAY

(2)

The performing instrument is_____.

ANSWER

cello

To be sure, the final three sixteenth notes in the pattern are unaccented. For the time being, however, only the third note of the four-note pattern will be discussed. Melodic direction change occurring on either the second or fourth notes will be treated later.

215 In this frame, the melody changes direction on an unaccented portion of a beat. Indicate the location with an arrow.

Press PLAY

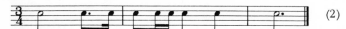 (2)

The performing instrument is_____.

ANSWER

trumpet
Make certain that you are conducting the metric beats and tapping the sixteenth-note divisions while you listen. Sing this melody before proceeding to the next frame.

---

216 There are two direction changes in this frame. One occurs on an unaccented portion of a beat.

Press PLAY

 (3)

The performing instrument is_____.

ANSWER

piano

---

217 In the next few frames, a portion of the melody will be omitted. Each omitted section will contain one or more melodic adaptions of the following sixteenth-note rhythmic patterns:

Conduct and tap while you listen. Determine rhythmic points of direction change before writing your response. Complete the omitted section.

Press PLAY

 (3)

The performing instrument is_____.

ANSWER

flute
Your response should have contained two points of direction change, both of which occurred on accented portions of the beats.

218   This melody begins on a note other than the tonic. Apply the procedure for locating the starting note while you listen.*

After listening to the melody, determine the rhythmic point of direction change. Do this *before* writing your response. Complete the omitted measure.

Press PLAY

(3)

The performing instrument is_____.

*See Frames 168 to 178 for a review of this procedure.

ANSWER

If you find that you need more presentations of each frame than the tape provides, be sure to rewind the tape for additional playings. It is important that you be convinced your answer is correct before you check your response with the correct answer. Sing this melody before proceeding to the next frame.

bassoon

---

219   Determine the rhythmic points of direction change before writing. Your response should contain two of the sixteenth-note rhythmic patterns.

Press PLAY

(3)

The performing instrument is_____.

ANSWER

clarinet

Always orient yourself to the printed music as much as is possible before listening to the recorded example.

220 This frame contains five concepts which have been discussed in the book thus far:

1. Location of starting note
2. Dotted-note rhythms
3. Sixteenth-note patterns
4. Change of melodic direction
5. Identification of performing instrument

Conduct and tap while you listen. After you can mentally sing this short melody, notate it.

Press PLAY

(3)

The performing instrument is_____.

trumpet

In the event you should change direction at incorrect points, you may find that your notation does not correspond to the tonal center. That is, you may be writing a degree or more from the correct notation, as in this example:

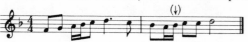

Always check your notation to be certain that it conforms to the tonal center you hear.

---

221 Follow as much of the "prelistening" process (see Frame 52) as possible for this frame. Write the entire melody.

Press PLAY

(3)

The performing instrument is_____.

ANSWER

flute

When you sing this melody, be sure to observe the rests in the first and last measures.

---

222 Write this melody.

Press PLAY

(3)

The performing instrument is_____.

ANSWER

piano

223   In the next few frames, the printed melody will differ from that which you hear. Be sure to sing the printed melody as a part of your "prelistening" process. Locate the difference and notate what is played.

Press PLAY

(3)

The performing instrument is_____ .

ANSWER

violin

Observe that the change of direction occurs on the accented portion of the first beat in the second measure. Sing this melody again as you heard it *played*.

---

224   The difference in this frame is similar to that in the preceding one.

Press PLAY

(3)

The performing instrument is_____ .

ANSWER

horn

225 The difference in this frame involves both pitch and rhythm.

Press PLAY

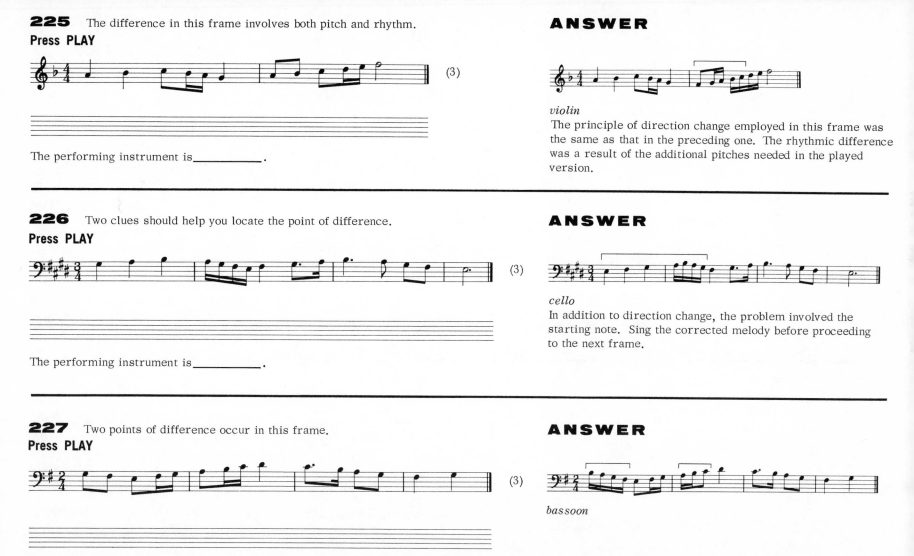

(3)

The performing instrument is_____.

ANSWER

violin

The principle of direction change employed in this frame was the same as that in the preceding one. The rhythmic difference was a result of the additional pitches needed in the played version.

226 Two clues should help you locate the point of difference.

Press PLAY

(3)

The performing instrument is_____.

ANSWER

cello

In addition to direction change, the problem involved the starting note. Sing the corrected melody before proceeding to the next frame.

227 Two points of difference occur in this frame.

Press PLAY

(3)

The performing instrument is_____.

ANSWER

bassoon

228 Change of melodic direction may occur on the second or fourth note of the sixteenth-note pattern (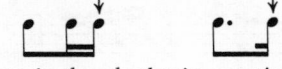 or).

Conduct the metric beat and tap the sixteen-note divisions while listening to this melody. It changes direction on a pattern. Sing along with the second playing.

Press PLAY

(2)

The performing instrument is _____ .

---

229 In addition to the 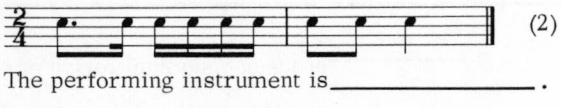 pattern, melodic direction change at this particular unaccented location of the beat may also take place in these patterns:

Place an arrow over the note in the rhythmic notation where you hear a change of melodic direction occur. It will be on the particular unaccented portion indicated above. Sing the melodic line before writing your response.

Press PLAY

(2)

The performing instrument is _____ .

230   In this frame, the melody changes direction on the fourth sixteenth-note division of the beat. Indicate the location with an arrow as in the preceding frame.

Press PLAY

(2)

The performing instrument is_____ .

ANSWER

piano

Always conduct the metric beats and tap the sixteenth-note divisions while you listen. Sing this melody again before proceeding to the next frame.

---

231   There are two direction changes in this frame. Only one will occur on the fourth sixteenth-note division of a beat. Indicate the locations of direction change with arrows.

Press PLAY

(3)

The performing instrument is_____ .

ANSWER

violin

---

232   In the next few frames, a portion of the melody will be omitted. Each omitted section will contain one or more melodic adaptations of the following sixteenth-note rhythmic patterns:

Melodic direction change on the fourth sixteenth-note division of the beat will be involved in this frame. Locate the rhythmic point of direction change before writing your response. Complete the omitted section.

Press PLAY

(2)

The performing instrument is_____ .

ANSWER

trumpet

233 This melody begins on a note other than the tonic. The omitted section contains a melodic direction change on the fourth sixteenth-note division of a beat.

Locate the rhythmic point of direction change before writing your response. Complete the omitted section.

Press PLAY

(3)

The performing instrument is_____.

ANSWER

horn

---

234 The omitted section contains two points of direction change. Locate these rhythmically before writing.

Press PLAY

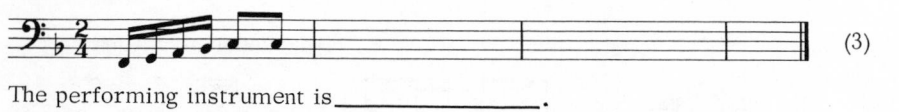

(3)

The performing instrument is_____.

ANSWER

bassoon
Sing this melody again before proceeding to the next frame.

---

235 Determine the rhythmic location of the direction changes and mentally sing this melody before writing your response.

Press PLAY

(3)

The performing instrument is_____ .

ANSWER

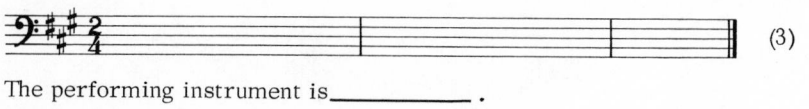

cello
Notice that the rhythm of measure 2 is that of measure 1. If you made this observation while listening you then were able to give your attention to the pitches.

236 Be alert for rests.

Press PLAY

(3)

The performing instrument is _____ .

ANSWER

violin

If you are having difficulty locating the rhythmic point of direction change, review:

Frames 210 to 227 for  and

Frames 228 to 236 for

---

237 In addition to melodic direction changes, the melody in this frame also contains syncopation. After you can mentally sing this short melody, write it.

Press PLAY

(3)

The performing instrument is _____ .

ANSWER

trombone

---

238 Listen for the rhythmic location of melodic direction change and for the location of rests.

Press PLAY

(3)

The performing instrument is _____ .

ANSWER

flute

239 In the next few frames, the printed melody will differ from that which you hear.

Observe carefully the key and meter signatures. Before listening, mentally sing the printed melody. Locate the two points of difference and write what is played in this frame.

Press PLAY

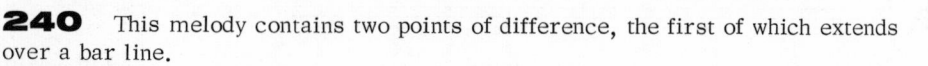

(3)

The performing instrument is_____ .

ANSWER

piano

---

240 This melody contains two points of difference, the first of which extends over a bar line.

Press PLAY

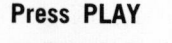

(3)

The performing instrument is_____ .

ANSWER

trumpet

If you had difficulty with the starting note, the rhythmic location of melodic direction change in the second measure should have provided a clue. The second difference required attention to duration of the tone. Sing the correct melody again before proceeding.

241 Locate and rewrite all points of difference in this frame.

Press PLAY

(3)

The performing instrument is_____.

TEST 4

Before proceeding with the program, complete the test items for Test 4, which will be found at the back of the book. Obtain the tape-recorded materials for this test from your instructor.

ANSWER

clarinet

If you made errors locating points of difference or writing what you heard at those points, listen to the performance once again. Follow the printed music of the correct answer, paying particular attention to the duration of notes and rhythmic location of melodic direction change. Sing the correct clarinet melody before proceeding to the next frame.

242 Press PLAY

All motion up to this time has been stepwise motion. However, most melodies contain some interval skips in the melodic line. At this point, you will begin to hear and see melodies containing skips.

Interval skips can occur in several ways. One frequent way in which they are found is when the melody outlines notes in the tonic triad. By this time, you are well acquainted with the tonic triad, since it is used to indicate the tonality of the melodies in these frames.

Listen to this portion of a melody. It contains interval skips which outline the notes in the tonic triad.

(1)

The performing instrument is_____ .

ANSWER

horn

243

In frame 167, melodies were introduced which began on notes other than the tonic. The procedure outlined at that point is one which now you should be doing consistently and effectively. The procedure makes it possible to more easily locate the starting note. It also makes it possible to keep track of the tonal center of the melodies while you listen to them.*

In the next few frames, the printed music will contain only the rhythmic notation of the melodies played. Bracket the notes which outline an interval skip and indicate the scale degrees of the interval as in this example.

Press PLAY

(1)

The performing instrument is_____ .

*Review Frames 168 to 178 if you are not sure of the procedure referred to.

ANSWER

bassoon

When you write your response in the following frames, you may use either numbers or *sol-fa* syllables. It is not necessary to use both.

244 This frame contains two interval skips involving 1 and 3 (do and mi).
Bracket the location of each interval skip and indicate which note in each is 1 (do)
and which is 3 (mi).

Press PLAY

(3)

The performing instrument is_____ .

ANSWER

flute

---

245 This frame contains an ascending (1-3) and a descending (3-1) interval
skip. Mentally sing the melody before making your response. Bracket and indicate
the notes as before.

Press PLAY

(3)

The performing instrument is_____ .

ANSWER

trombone

Observe that this melody did not begin on beat 1. Rhythmically
beginning a melody this way is referred to as starting on the
"up beat." The technical term is *anacrusis*. Sing this melody
again before proceeding to the next frame.

---

246 Follow the same procedure again in this frame.

Press PLAY

(3)

The performing instrument is_____ .

ANSWER

trumpet

Notice that all three interval skips were descending ones.

247 One of the interval skips in this frame will be between 5 and 3 (sol and mi). Listen particularly to these two notes while the tonic triad is being played. Bracket and indicate notes as before.

Press PLAY

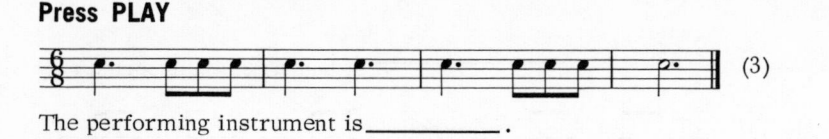

(3)

The performing instrument is_____.

ANSWER

cello

---

248 Follow the same procedure again in this frame.

Press PLAY

(3)

The performing instrument is_____.

ANSWER

horn

It is important to be able to sing the melody to yourself after having heard it played once or twice. This makes it possible to slow the tempo mentally. In turn, this should make it easier to analyze the melody.

249 In the next few frames, the printed music will differ from that which you hear. Bracket the points of difference and write what you hear played.

The differences in this frame will be pitch differences and will involve interval skips. Sing the printed melody *before* you listen, in order to compare it with that which is played.

Press PLAY

(3)

The performing instrument is_____ .

ANSWER

bassoon
If you made an error:
1. Correct your written response.
2. Follow the printed melody in the response section while listening to another presentation of this frame on tape. Pay particular attention to the bracketed locations in order to observe the character of the difference.

---

250 This frame contains both rhythmic and melodic differences. Sing the printed music before listening. Bracket and rewrite as before.

Press PLAY

(3)

The performing instrument is_____ .

ANSWER

violin
The syncopation should have provided the clue to the correct response. Sing the corrected melody before proceeding to the next frame.

251 Determine points of difference and rewrite.

Press PLAY

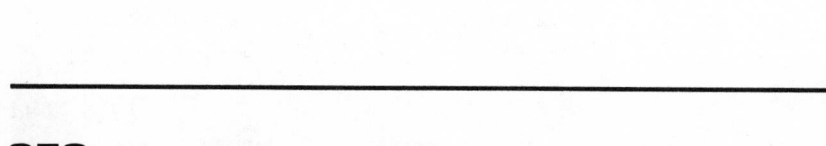

(3)

The performing instrument is_____ .

ANSWER

piano

Earlier in the program, reference was made to the leading tone as a means to help maintain a focus on the tonal center. The notes of the tonic triad can also serve to provide this focus. The final note of the second measure illustrates this.

Listen to this melody once more and observe the prominence of the tonic triad notes marked *. Continue to sing the corrected melodies in each frame before proceeding to the next.

252 Locate differences and rewrite as before.

Press PLAY

(3)

The performing instrument is_____ .

ANSWER

clarinet

Notice the different concepts involved in your responses which have been discussed previously:

1. Starting pitch (measure 1)
2. Rhythmic location of melodic direction change (measure 3)
3. Interval skips (measures 1 and 3)

253 In the next few frames, a portion of the printed melody will be omitted. Your written response should contain interval skips using only notes found in the tonic triad. Follow these steps:

1. Observe key and meter signatures.
2. Locate starting note.
3. Sing the melody you hear.
4. Listen for interval skips and identify them.
5. Be alert to rhythmic elements used.
6. Complete the omitted measures.

Press PLAY

(3)

The performing instrument is_____.

ANSWER

cello

---

254 Only the second measure is printed in this frame. Follow the steps outlined in the preceding frame.

Press PLAY

(3)

The performing instrument is_____.

ANSWER

trombone

---

255 Complete the omitted measures.

Press PLAY

(3)

The performing instrument is_____.

ANSWER

horn
Any problem with rests? If so, listen again with attention to duration.

256 Complete the omitted measures.

Press PLAY

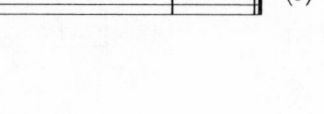

(3)

The performing instrument is _____ .

ANSWER

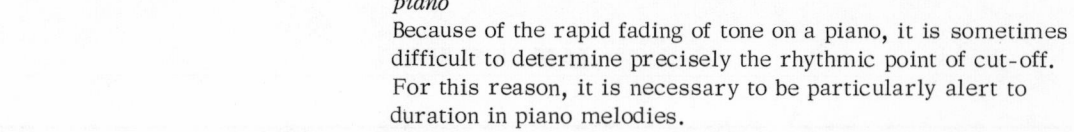

piano
Because of the rapid fading of tone on a piano, it is sometimes difficult to determine precisely the rhythmic point of cut-off. For this reason, it is necessary to be particularly alert to duration in piano melodies.

---

257 Until now, interval skips have been confined to 1-3 (do-mi) and 3-5 (mi-sol).
  Listen to the sound of a melodic line containing the interval skip between 1-5 (do-sol).
  Sing along with the second playing.

Press PLAY

(2)

The performing instrument is _____ .

ANSWER

bassoon

---

258 In this frame, the melody contains a skip between 1-5 (do-sol).
  While listening to the melody, rhythmically locate this interval (1-5) before writing your response. Complete the omitted section.

Press PLAY

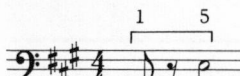

(3)

The performing instrument is _____ .

ANSWER

cello

259 The omitted section in this frame contains an interval skip.

Press PLAY

(3)

The performing instrument is_____ .

ANSWER

flute

---

260 In the preceding two frames, the interval skip between 1-5 was either *up* to 5 or *down* to 1. The reverse direction is also possible, as you well know.

Observe the melodic movement of 5 *up* to 1 in the first measure of this melody while you listen.

Be able to mentally sing this melody before making your response. Try to do this in one or two hearings if possible. Complete the omitted section.

Press PLAY

(3)

The performing instrument is_____ .

ANSWER

trumpet

It is important to learn to make your responses with as few hearings as possible. Remember, in most instances we have only *one* opportunity to hear unless we are listening to a recording and choose to play it over several times.

If you find it necessary in this program of study, listen more often for the sake of accuracy.

---

261 Complete the omitted measures.

Press PLAY

(3)

The performing instrument is_____ .

ANSWER

trombone

262   Write this melody.

Press PLAY

(3)

The performing instrument is_____.

ANSWER

violin

---

263   Earlier frames used the sixteenth note in simple meter. This frame contains the sixteenth note in compound meter. A frequently encountered compound pattern which uses a sixteenth note is found in the bracketed sections in this frame.

   The melody will be played twice. Conduct the metric beats while you listen to the first playing. Conduct and sing along with the second.

Press PLAY

(2)

The performing instrument is_____.

ANSWER

clarinet

---

264   In this and the next frame, a portion of the printed music will be omitted. The rhythm of the omitted section will be either ♪♪♪ or ♪.♪♪ .

Press PLAY

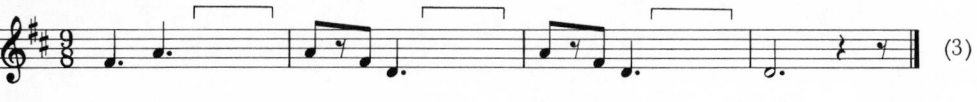

(3)

The performing instrument is_____.

ANSWER

trumpet

There is very little possibility of confusing the ♪.♪♪ pattern with any compound pattern other than ♪♪♪, since these two are the only ones studied thus far which contain three notes. Sing this melody before proceeding.

265 Follow the same procedure in this frame. Use either ♩♪♩ or ♩.♪♩ to complete the bracketed sections. Each bracketed section constitutes a metric beat.

Press PLAY

(3)

The performing instrument is_____ .

ANSWER

piano

---

266 In the next few frames, a portion of the melody will not be printed. Complete the omitted section with one or more of the following rhythmic patterns:

(Of course, you are to use the correct pitches.)

Press PLAY

(3)

The performing instrument is_____ .

ANSWER

flute

---

267 Your response to this frame will involve five of the rhythmic patterns listed in the preceding frame. Be alert for interval skips.

Press PLAY

(3)

The performing instrument is_____ .

ANSWER

horn

268 Write this melody.

Press PLAY

(3)

The performing instrument is_____ .

ANSWER

cello
Notice that two eighth rests were used in the third measure, rather than a quarter rest. This is a standard procedure in music notation with compound meter. When you sing this melody, be sure to observe the rests.

---

269 Bracket the five points of difference between the printed music and that which you hear. One difference will be melodic. Rewrite the melody correctly on the second staff.

Press PLAY

(3)

The performing instrument is_____ .

ANSWER

clarinet
Rhythmic location of melodic direction change was the clue to the difference on beat 3 of the first measure. The next frame will involve a similar listening problem.

270   Before listening to this frame's melody:
  1. Examine the key and meter signatures.
  2. Mentally sing the printed melody.
After you have done this, listen to the recording and compare your sung version with the played one. Be sure to listen a sufficient number of times.

Press PLAY

(3)

The performing instrument is_____.

violin

Observe how an awareness of the rhythmic point of direction change can reinforce your knowledge of pitch differences in the first measure. If you are having difficulty detecting the difference between ♩♩♩ and ♩.♩♩, review Frames 263 to 269 before proceeding.

---

271   Locate and rewrite differences as before.

Press PLAY

(3)

The performing instrument is_____.

ANSWER

bassoon

Sing the corrected melody before proceeding.

272 In the preceding frames, interval skips between 1-3 have been *up* to 3 and *down* to 1. As you know, it is possible to skip from 3 *up* to 1, and vice versa.

Listen to this excerpt from a familiar melody. Sing along with the second playing.

Press PLAY

(2)

The performing instrument is_____ .

ANSWER

trombone

---

273 The omitted section in this frame contains an interval skip of 3 *up* to 1. Be able to sing the melody before writing your response.

Press PLAY

(3)

The performing instrument is_____ .

ANSWER

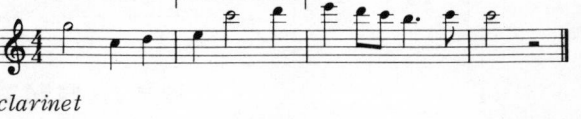

clarinet

---

274 Your response should contain two interval skips.

Press PLAY

(3)

The performing instrument is_____ .

ANSWER

piano

It is important to maintain the tonic triad in your memory while you listen, particularly in melodies containing interval skips. Observe the 1 *down* to 3 interval in the third measure. Sing this melody again while following the printed music.

275 Examine the printed music. Observe that the final note is 5. After listening, be able to sing the melody before writing your response.

Press PLAY

(3)

The performing instrument is _____ .

ANSWER

horn

---

276 Complete the omitted section.

Press PLAY

(3)

The performing instrument is _____ .

ANSWER

trumpet

Did you observe that measure 3 was the same as measure 1? This recognition of repetition is a useful technique in aural perception.

---

277 Write this melody. Be alert to rests.

Press PLAY

(3)

The performing instrument is _____ .

ANSWER

cello

278 Press PLAY

Earlier, syncopation was defined as notes beginning on unaccented parts of the beat tied over to notes on the accented part of the beat, thus producing a shift of accent. Eighth notes were used to illustrate this, as in the following illustration. Conduct the beat while you listen.

 (1)

The performing instrument is_____.

ANSWER

flute

---

279 Press PLAY

To illustrate how the feeling of syncopation is written using sixteenth notes, compare the original version of the preceding frame's melody with the same melody in

$\frac{2}{4}$ written in two measures.

  The bracketed section illustrates another way to notate syncopation using sixteenth notes.

 (1)

 (1)

The performing instrument is_____.

ANSWER

flute

280   The omitted section contains a syncopated sixteenth-note figure.

Press PLAY

(3)

The performing instrument is_____.

ANSWER

trombone

Be careful to conduct the metric beat vigorously while you listen. This has been found to be particularly helpful in locating shift of accent. Sing this melody again while conducting the beat. Listen again to the tape if necessary.

---

281   Conduct the metric beat while listening to this melody. Try to sing the melody after one or two hearings if possible.

Press PLAY

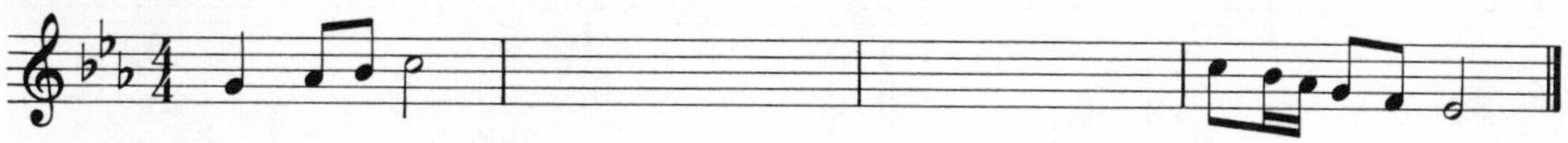

(3)

The performing instrument is_____.

ANSWER

violin

---

282   Write this melody.

Press PLAY

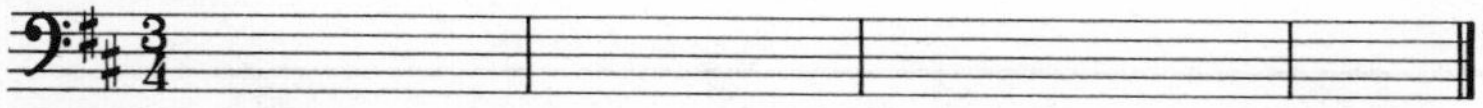

(3)

The performing instrument is_____.

ANSWER

bassoon

If you used a syncopated sixteenth-note figure in your response you could not have been too conscious of your conducting. If you made no errors, you are well on your way.

283 Write this melody.
Press PLAY

(3)

The performing instrument is_____.

ANSWER

trumpet

---

284 Locate and rewrite the differences in the following frames.
 This frame has three points of difference. Examine the printed music carefully before listening. Include singing the printed music as part of your examination.
Press PLAY

(3)

The performing instrument is_____.

ANSWER

cello

---

285 Follow the same procedure again in this frame.
Press PLAY

(3)

The performing instrument is_____.

ANSWER

horn

Sing the melody again as it is printed in the response section. After you have done this, play the tape again and sing the melody which was played. Conduct the metric beat while you do this.

286 Syncopation can be found in compound meter, as well as in simple meter. There are several compound rhythmic patterns which are syncopated. Perhaps the most frequent is the type found in the bracketed sections of the melody in this frame. Observe that the shift of accent now is obtained by tying the last two eighth notes, ♪♪♪ , together.

  Conduct the metric beat and tap the divisions while you listen. Sing along with the second playing.

Press PLAY

The performing instrument is_____.

ANSWER

violin
The syncopated rhythmic figure ♪♪♪ is usually written ♪♩ .

287 Locate and rewrite differences in this frame. Compound syncopation will be involved.
Press PLAY

(3)

The performing instrument is _____ .

ANSWER

bassoon

Be sure that you examine the printed music in frames such as this *before* you listen. Sing the printed music in order to facilitate comparison with the performance.

Because the figure ♪♩ is the same as ♩♪♩ , tapping the compound divisions of the metric beat may prove to be helpful in recognizing this syncopated figure.

---

288 Rewrite the points of difference as you hear them played.
Press PLAY

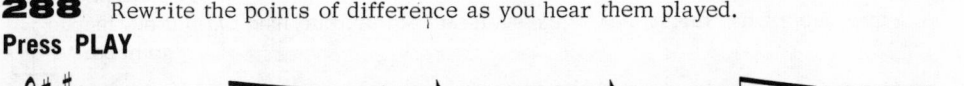

(3)

The performing instrument is _____ .

ANSWER

piano

289   A syncopated pattern will be used in your written response. Conduct the beat vigorously while you listen. Sing the melody played before writing your response.

Press PLAY

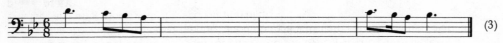

(3)

The performing instrument is_____.

ANSWER

trombone
The repetition in measure 3 of the rhythm pattern of measure 2 should have been one of the musical elements which you observed. If you did not, sing the melody again, giving particular attention to the rhythmic repetition.

---

290   In addition to the omitted second measure, two metric beats have been omitted from the first measure of the printed music. Complete this printed melody.

Press PLAY

(3)

The performing instrument is_____.

ANSWER

clarinet

---

291   Another syncopated compound figure is the ♪♪♩♪♪ pattern. Conduct the beat vigorously while listening to this syncopated melody. Conduct and sing along with the second playing.

Press PLAY

(2)

The performing instrument is_____.

ANSWER

trumpet
Conduct and sing this melody several times to get the "feel" of this particular pattern.

292 The omitted measure can be completed with a  pattern. All you need to do is supply the correct pitches.

Press PLAY

(3)

The performing instrument is_____.

ANSWER

violin

---

293 Both types of syncopated compound patterns studied thus far (♪ ♩ and

) will be used in your response in this frame.

Press PLAY

(3)

The performing instrument is_____.

ANSWER

bassoon

In addition to checking your syncopation, be sure that your interval skips were accurately notated in the third measure.

---

294 In earlier compound-rhythm frames, change of melodic direction was limited to the accented portion of the beat (♪♪♪) or on the final division (♪♪♪).

Change of direction on ♪♪♪ can be easily detected by relating the change to the syncopated figure ♪♪♪ (♪ ♪).

Observe the melodic direction change in the bracketed section. While you are listening to it played, relate the point of change to the syncopated figure suggested. Conducting the metric beat and tapping the divisions will help establish this relation. Conduct and sing along with the second playing.

Press PLAY

(2)

The performing instrument is *cello*.

ANSWER

No written response required. Proceed to the next frame.

295 The omitted section will contain melodic direction changes occurring on

the ♩♩♩ portion of the beat.

Press PLAY

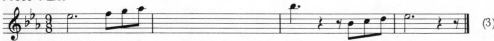

The performing instrument is_____.

(3)

ANSWER

flute

Sing this melody again, giving attention to the interval skip of an octave. The next frame will involve an octave skip in your response.

---

296 Complete the omitted section.

Press PLAY

The performing instrument is_____.

(3)

ANSWER

horn

---

297 Complete the omitted section.

Press PLAY

The performing instrument is_____.

(3)

ANSWER

clarinet

298 When you examine the music in this frame, observe the rhythmic location of direction change indicated by the arrow. Previously, direction changes on 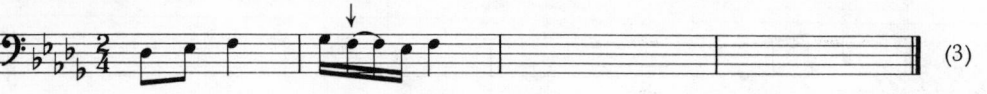,

and were discussed.

The point of change in this frame can be related to the syncopated pattern .

The omitted section contains two interval skips. Be alert for the location and kind.

Press PLAY

(3)

The performing instrument is _____ .

ANSWER

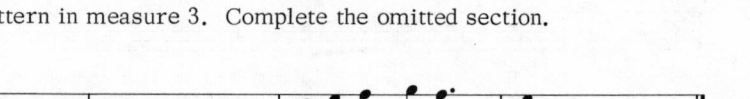

bassoon

---

299 Another syncopated rhythmic figure in simple meter is . This is like the pattern in that the accent shift is to the second sixteenth note division. Observe the . pattern in measure 3. Complete the omitted section.

Press PLAY

(3)

The performing instrument is _____ .

ANSWER

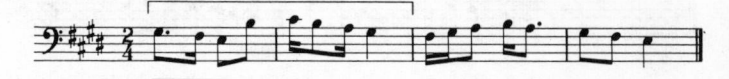

trombone

If you had difficulty with the rhythmic point of direction change, listen especially for this and mark its location with an arrow before writing your response. Continue to conduct the beat vigorously, both while listening and while mentally singing the melodies.

---

300 The omitted section contains a . pattern. All interval skips are from and to notes found in the tonic triad. All other motion will be stepwise.

Press PLAY

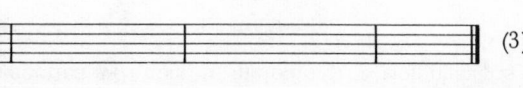 (3)

The performing instrument is _____ .

ANSWER

piano

301   Here are both syncopation and interval skips in compound meter.

Press PLAY

(3)

The performing instrument is_____.

ANSWER

flute

Play this melody again if necessary to be sure that you can mentally sing it accurately.   Conduct the beat while you sing.

---

302   This melody combines the two *compound* syncopated patterns studied.

Press PLAY

(3)

The performing instrument is_____.

ANSWER

horn

---

303   Complete the omitted section.

Press PLAY

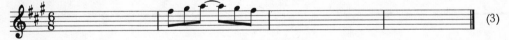

(3)

The performing instrument is_____.

ANSWER

violin

The pattern  found in measure 3 of this melody, and in Frame 302, is an introduction to the pattern to be presented in the next frame. Sing this melody again. Conduct the metric beat while you sing.

304 The syncopated pattern referred to in the preceding frame is that illustrated in the bracketed sections of the melody in this frame. The musical name for this rhythmic pattern is *hemiola*.

Listen to this frame twice. Conduct the metric beats (indicated by the arrows). Conduct and sing along with the second playing.

Press PLAY

(2)

ANSWER

The rhythm pattern found in the second and third measures is usually notated in any of the manners indicated. The use of ties was to focus your attention on the rhythmic location of the accent shifts.

305 Bracket and rewrite points of difference in the next few frames. The difference in this frame involves hemiola (♩ ♪♪).

Press PLAY

(3)

The performing instrument is_____ .

ANSWER

trumpet
Are you following your "prelistening" routine? Carefully examine the printed music in the response sections before listening.

306 This frame contains differences of both rhythm and pitch.
Press PLAY

The performing instrument is_____ .

(3)

trombone

You may have used a quarter rest (♩) instead of two eighth rests (♪ ♪); however, the latter is preferred. If you had difficulty with this frame, review those concepts on which you made your error.

---

307 Bracket differences and rewrite.
Press PLAY

The performing instrument is_____ .

(3)

ANSWER

cello

---

308 Hemiola is used in the omitted section. Listen also for interval skips.
Press PLAY

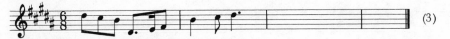

The performing instrument is_____ .

(3)

ANSWER

piano

Your answer is still correct if you wrote ♩♩♩ instead of ♩ ♪♪♩ for measure 3.

309   Complete the omitted section. Your response will need a syncopated rhythmic figure.
Press PLAY

The performing instrument is_____ .

ANSWER

bassoon
When you sing this melody again, observe the staccato feeling in the last measure.

---

310   Complete the first two measures.
Press PLAY

The performing instrument is_____ .

ANSWER

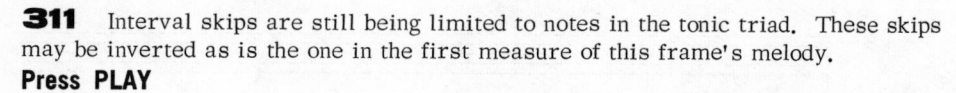

horn
If you are having trouble perceiving hemiola, review Frames 304 to 309 before proceeding.

   Take notice of the rhythmic location of the final tonic note. It occurs on an unaccented portion of a beat and is tied over, creating a syncopated effect. Be alert for similar treatments in forthcoming frames.

---

311   Interval skips are still being limited to notes in the tonic triad. These skips may be inverted as is the one in the first measure of this frame's melody.
Press PLAY

The performing instrument is_____ .

ANSWER

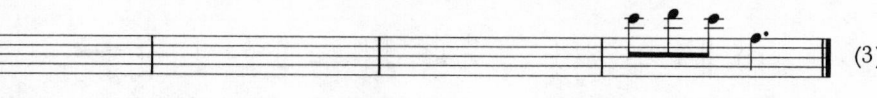

piano
Did the word "inverted" puzzle you? If 3 *down* to 1 were the natural (or normal) position of the interval (and it is), then 3 *up* to 1 would be considered an *inverted* position.

312 Try writing this melody in compound rhythm. Be careful to use the right number of leger lines.

Press PLAY

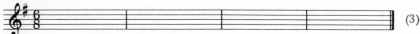

(3)

The performing instrument is_____.

ANSWER

flute

---

313 The next several frames are included to review concepts discussed in the program thus far. No new concepts will be introduced in these frames. If you have difficulty with a particular concept, check the Index for the frame number where that concept was introduced.

Listen to each melody as often as needed to ensure accuracy of response. Attempt to accurately respond in three or less hearings if possible.

Press PLAY

(3)

The performing instrument is_____.

ANSWER

violin

Concepts involved in this frame:
1. Starting note other than tonic
2. Interval skips
3. Syncopation
4. Melodic direction change
5. Dotted rhythms
6. Timbre discrimination

---

314 Write this melody in three hearings or less if at all possible. Being able to sing the melody accurately after one or two hearings will make this possible. Take as little time between hearings as you can and yet be confident of what you heard.

Press PLAY

(3)

The performing instrument is_____.

ANSWER

trombone

This frame involved the concept of rests.

315 Write this melody in as few hearings as possible.

Press PLAY

(3)

The performing instrument is_____ .

ANSWER

trumpet

---

316 If you are able to sing this after one or two hearings, the chances for accuracy of your written response will be increased.

Press PLAY

(3)

The performing instrument is_____ .

ANSWER

clarinet
Notice the melodic direction change on 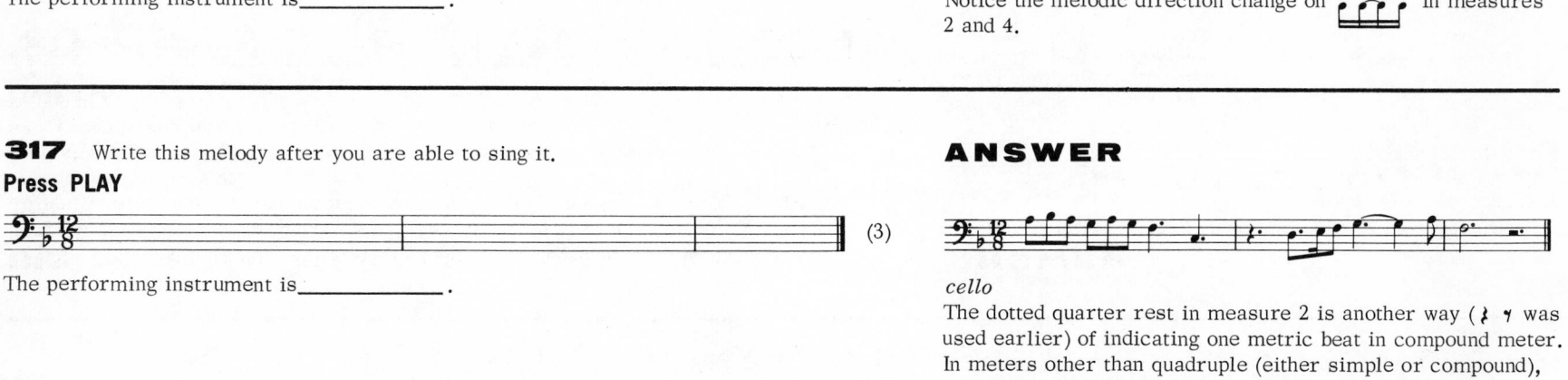 in measures 2 and 4.

---

317 Write this melody after you are able to sing it.

Press PLAY

(3)

The performing instrument is_____ .

ANSWER

cello
The dotted quarter rest in measure 2 is another way (𝄾 𝄿 was used earlier) of indicating one metric beat in compound meter. In meters other than quadruple (either simple or compound), the whole rest (▬) is used to signify an entire measure's rest. The next frame will illustrate this.

318 Be alert for rests.
Press PLAY

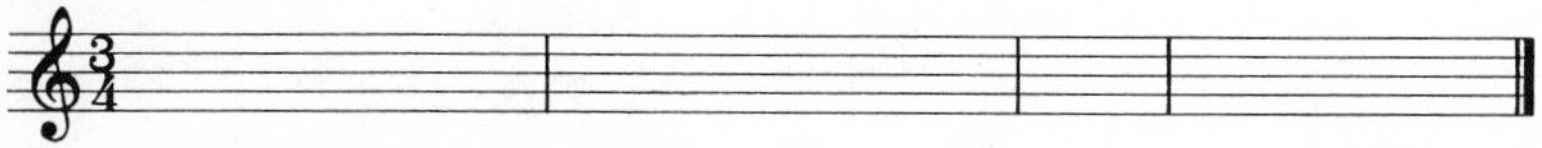

The performing instrument is _____ .

ANSWER

horn

---

319 Write this melody.
Press PLAY

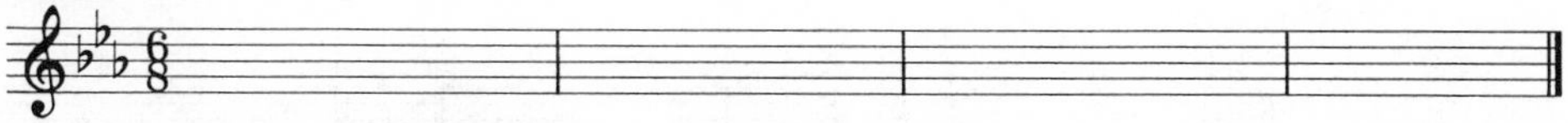

The performing instrument is _____ .

ANSWER

flute

♩ ♪ is not the same as ♫ ♪ ♩ . Be careful to discriminate between the two.

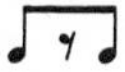

TEST 6
Before proceeding with the program, complete the test items for Test 6, which will be found at the back of the book. Obtain the tape-recorded materials for this test from your instructor.

320 Press PLAY

Until this point in the program, all melodies have been in the major mode; that is, all notes used in the melodies have been taken from the major scale of the key in which the melody was written. Listen to the two melodies in this frame. The first is in the major mode and the second is in minor mode.

(1)

(1)

ANSWER

For the time being, no written response to instrument identification will be required. Periodic frames will be used later in the program to provide review for this skill. This section will concentrate on presentation of minor melodies.

---

321 Press PLAY

There are three common forms of minor scales. The first one which will be considered is the natural minor scale. Listen to this natural minor scale in the key of A. Observe the half-step relation indicated by (∧) between the second and third degrees of the scale.

1 2 3 4 5 6 7 1 7 6 5 4 3 2 1

(1)

ANSWER

The interval distance between 1 and 3 is narrower by one-half step in minor than it is in major. Observe this difference when listening to the preparatory tonic triad. In the minor mode, this interval (1-3) is called a minor third. In the major mode, it is called a major third.

322 Press PLAY

In the natural form of minor, there are no accidentals. It is from the natural minor that the key signature for minor scales is obtained. Observe that in the A minor scale, there are no sharps or flats. The key of C major also has no sharps or flats.

As you listen to these two scales, notice that scale degrees 1 *up* to 6 in major are identical with scale degrees 3 *up* to 1 in minor.

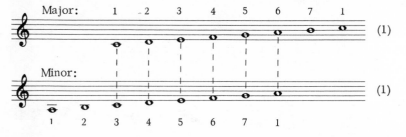

ANSWER

In this frame, a major scale with C as its tonic and a minor scale with A as its tonic were played. These two scales (C major and A minor) are *related* because they both use the same key signature.

---

323 This and the next frame will contain no recorded material. Do not press PLAY until instructed to do so.

Because there is a relationship between a major and a minor key which use the same key signature, we refer to such keys as *relative* keys.

A minor and C major use the same key signature. Because of this, C major could be called the _____ major of A minor.

ANSWER

relative
You may have written *related* for your response. This would have been accurate. However, the common terminology is *relative* major or *relative* minor.

---

324 Look at Frame 322 again. Notice that the tonic of the A minor scale is the same note as the *sixth* degree of the C major scale. The *sixth* degree of any major scale is always the same note as the tonic of a minor scale having the *same key signature* as that major scale.

Bracket the note of this G major scale which would be the same note as the tonic of a minor scale with the same key signature (one sharp).

ANSWER

E was the correct note. Because of this, it can be concluded that the key signature of one sharp is *either* G major or E minor. It could be said that G is the *relative major* of E minor or one might say that E is the *relative minor* of G major.

325 When reference is made to *relative* major or *relative* minor, it means that one key signature can indicate either a major key or a minor key.

In the next two frames refer to the major scale written on the first staff.

1. Bracket the sixth degree of the major scale.
2. Using the bracketed note as tonic, write a natural minor scale on the second staff.
3. Check your response with the correct answer.

Do not Press PLAY yet

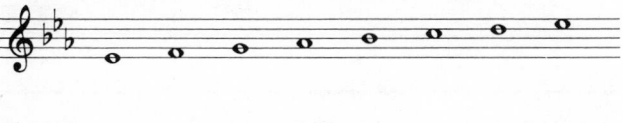

ANSWER

Your answer should have contained a clef, the correct key signature, and the correct notation of C minor in any octave. If you used accidentals, remember that the *natural* minor uses no accidentals. After you have corrected any errors, press PLAY and listen to the clarinet play this *natural* minor scale in C.

---

326 Follow the same procedure again in this frame:

1. Bracket the sixth degree of the printed major scale.
2. Write a natural minor scale using the bracketed note as the tonic.
3. Check your written response.

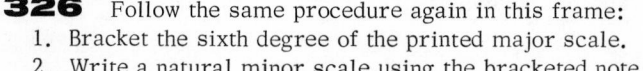

ANSWER

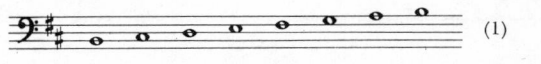

If you wrote the B minor scale in a different octave, that does not matter. The answer printed does correspond to the one which is recorded. After listening to the B minor scale played, sing it before proceeding.

Press PLAY

327 Follow the same procedure again in this frame.

ANSWER

 (1)

If you have had difficulty with Frames 324 to 327, review these with your instructor before proceeding. Sing this scale after hearing it played.

Press PLAY

---

328 In the following frames, a clef and key signature will be given. The performing instrument will play either a major or a minor scale corresponding to the key signature. Determine the mode (whether major or minor) and write the scale you hear played.

Press PLAY

The scale is_____(major, minor).

(1)

ANSWER

major

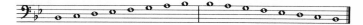

If you wrote a minor scale, listen to this frame again and observe the presence of a leading tone. The natural minor does not have this. In addition, listen to the major third between 1-3 (two whole steps).

---

329 Listen for the treatment of the third degree as well as for a leading-tone effect. After you have determined whether the scale is major or minor (i.e., the modality), write it down. Be sure that you write it correctly in the octave played.

Press PLAY

The scale is_____ .

(1)

ANSWER

minor

In this scale, you should have heard the half-step relationship between the second and third degrees. This creates a minor third between 1-3. Also, you should have been aware of the whole step between 7 and 1 (no leading-tone effect). Sing this scale before proceeding.

330 Follow the same procedure in this frame.

Press PLAY

The scale is_____ .

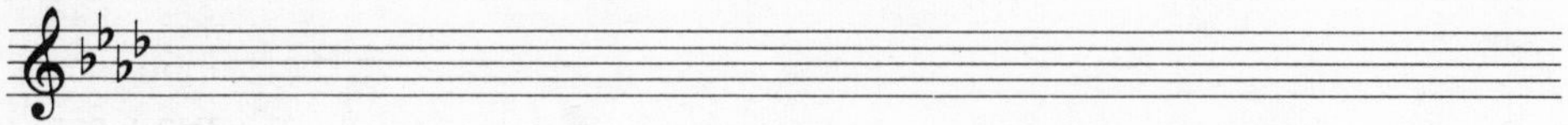

(1)

ANSWER

minor

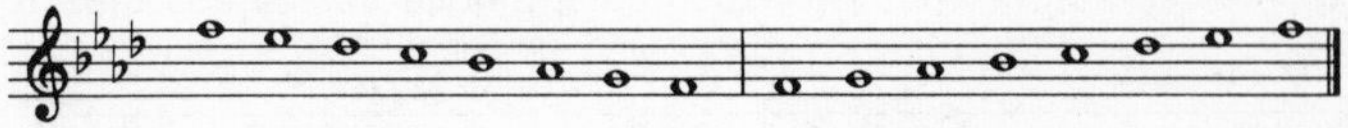

331 Write the scale you hear played. Indicate modality.

Press PLAY

The scale is_____ .

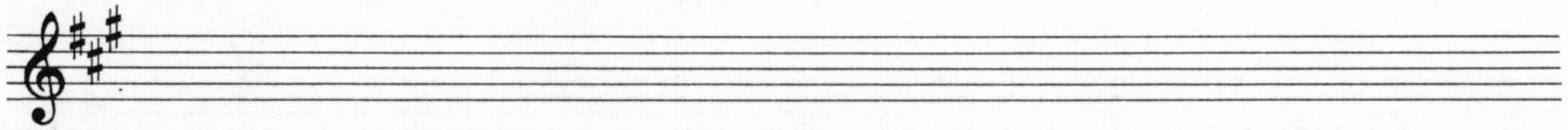

(1)

ANSWER

major

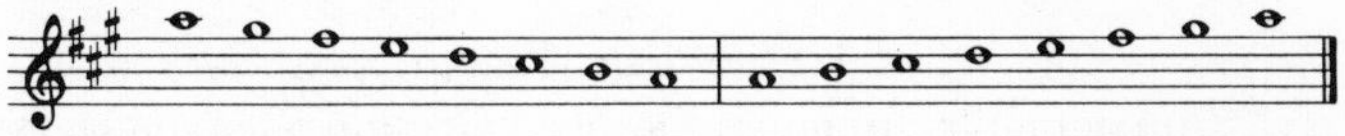

332 Follow the same procedure once again.

Press PLAY

The scale is_____ .

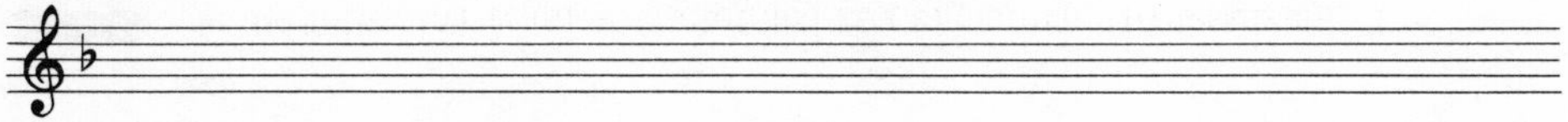

(1)

ANSWER

minor

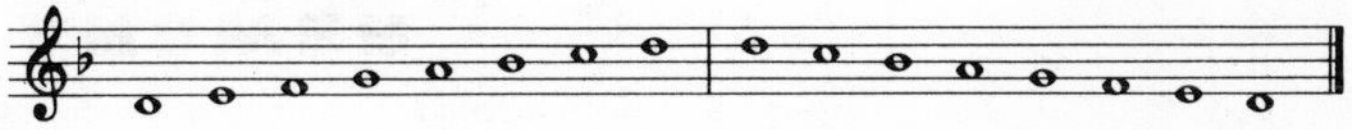

333   In the next few frames you are to write the ascending natural minor scale indicated, using the correct key signature. The natural minor scale to write for this frame is on B. To get the correct key signature, figure out which major scale has B as its sixth degree.

Do not Press PLAY yet

B minor:

ANSWER

(1)

After you have corrected any errors, follow this procedure:
1. Listen to the tonic triad played.
2. Sing the natural minor scale printed above during the period of silence after the tonic triad.
3. Compare your sung version with the played one.

Press PLAY

---

334   Another way to figure out which key signature to use for minor is to count *up* a minor third from the minor tonic. Use the major key signature for the note you end up with. For example, in the preceding frame, your minor key was B. Counting up a minor third, you obtain the note D. The key signature for D major is two sharps. Two sharps is also the key signature for B minor. Write a natural minor scale in G using a key signature. (Notice the clef.)

Do not press PLAY

G minor:

ANSWER

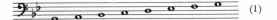

(1)

If you made an error, determine the cause and correct it. Listen to tonic triad, immediately sing the scale, and compare with the played version.

Press PLAY

---

335   Write a natural minor scale on C sharp using a key signature.

Do not press PLAY

C sharp minor:

ANSWER

(1)

After you have corrected any errors, sing and compare as before.

Press PLAY

336 Write a natural minor scale on B flat.

Do not press PLAY

B flat minor:

ANSWER

(1)

If you are having difficulty with this type of problem, review Frames 328 to 336 with your instructor before proceeding. Sing and compare this scale as before.

Press PLAY

---

337 Earlier, this program discussed the relationship which exists between a major scale and a minor scale that have the same key signature in common. Scales with this relationship are called relative major or relative minor scales.

Examine this scale. This scale is the_____ major scale of _____ minor.

ANSWER

relative; F

---

338 The parallel minor or parallel major is the name of another relationship which exists between major and minor scales. The minor scale having the *same tonic* as a major scale is referred to as the parallel minor of that particular major scale.

Examine this natural minor scale.

This natural minor scale is the_____ minor of G major.

ANSWER

parallel

339 Examine these two scales.

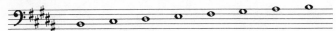

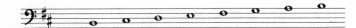

These are called *parallel* scales because both have the same _____ .

ANSWER

tonic

---

340 On the basis of information contained in the preceding frames, indicate the relationship of these two scales.

The scales are _____ (relative, parallel) because they have the same

_____ .

ANSWER

relative; key signatures

341 Press PLAY

You have become aware by this time of a difference in sound between the major and minor scales on the third degree. Listen particularly to the first five notes of the E major scale and compare with the first five notes of its parallel E minor scale. Notice the location of the half-step interval indicated by the sign (∧).

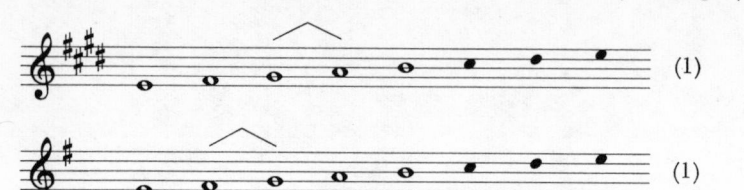

(1)

(1)

The pattern of the first five notes on the second staff is that of *all* minor scales.

ANSWER

Sing both scales. Be careful to sing accurately the first half step which is indicated in each.

342

In the next few frames, melodies will be played comprised only of the first five pitches of either the major or minor scale. Concentrate your attention on the treatment of the third degree of the scale as it is found in the melody. Write whether the melody you hear is major or minor.

Press PLAY

This melody is_____(major, minor).   (1)

ANSWER

minor

343

Listen for the location of the half-step interval. Indicate whether this melody is major or minor.

Press PLAY

This melody is_____(major, minor).   (1)

ANSWER

minor

344 Indicate the modality of this melody.

Press PLAY

This melody is _____ (major, minor). (1)

ANSWER

major

---

345 Indicate the modality.

Press PLAY

This melody is _____ (major, minor). (1)

ANSWER

minor

Conduct the beat vigorously as you sing in order to aid accurate performance of the hemiola in measures 2 and 3.

---

346 In the following frames, minor melodies will be played. A portion of the melody will not be printed. Complete the omitted portion after you are able to sing the melody played.

Press PLAY

 (3)

ANSWER

After correcting any errors, sing the melody played.

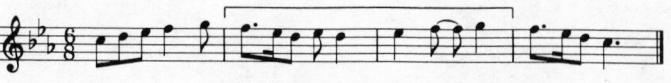

347 The omitted measures each contain syncopation. There are no interval skips.

Press PLAY

(3)

ANSWER

Be alert to rhythmic points of melodic direction change while you listen. If you are having difficulty feeling the syncopation in compound meter, be sure to conduct a vigorous metric beat. Tap the divisions of the beat if you find this helpful in syncopation.

---

348 At the present time, the melodies in minor mode contain only the first five notes of the minor scale. Try to sing this melody after one or two hearings. Complete the omitted section.

Press PLAY

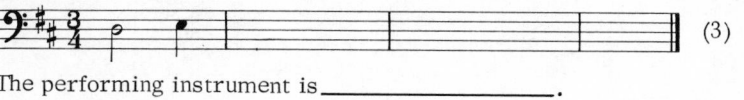

(3)

The performing instrument is _____ .

ANSWER

bassoon

---

349 Complete the omitted measures.

Press PLAY

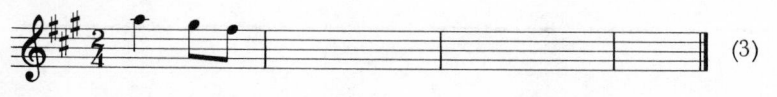

(3)

ANSWER

If you made an error, sing the correct melody again, comparing it while you sing with *your* written response. Observe the nature of the differences between the two. Play this frame's melody again if necessary.

350 The omitted measures are at the beginning of this melody. The routine for determining the starting note in minor melodies is the same as that for major ones. Complete the omitted section.

Press PLAY

 (3)

ANSWER

If you had difficulty with the starting note, mentally sing the tonic triad while it is being sounded. Use the numbers 1-3-5-3-1 for this.

---

351 Complete the omitted section after you can sing it.

Press PLAY

 (3)

ANSWER

Conduct the metric beat while you sing this melody again. "Feel" the syncopated shift of accent in the second measure.

---

352 In the next few frames, short melodies containing only the first five notes of a major or minor scale will be played. The printed music will omit the key signature. Write in the key signature which will indicate that the melody is major or minor.

Press PLAY

 (2)

ANSWER

Observe that the half-step interval was between the third and fourth degrees and not the second and third. This melody was in major modality.

353 This melody will have a key signature of either one flat or four flats.

Press PLAY

(2)

ANSWER

After you have determined the modality, follow the procedure for finding the key signature. Major key signatures should be no problem at this point. If you are having difficulty with minor key signatures, review Frames 320 to 341.

---

354 Write the appropriate key signature.

Press PLAY

(2)

ANSWER

---

355 Of the first five scale degrees, only the third indicates the modality. Observe how late in this melody you must wait before determining the mode. Locate the one occurence of the third before listening. Write the appropriate key signature.

Press PLAY

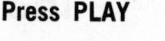 

(2)

ANSWER

The F sharp and B natural in the first measure would indicate that the melody was not in a B flat key. If you made that error—well!

Sing this melody again, but with the next to the last note (the third of the scale) as a D natural, in order to hear how this melody would sound in minor.

356 In the next few frames, short melodies will be played in either major or minor modality. Each will end on the tonic, but may begin on 1, 3, or 5. The printed music will contain the key and meter signatures. In each frame, (1) determine the mode and (2) write the last note (the tonic) played, as in this example.

Press PLAY

 (1)

ANSWER

When writing the tonic (the last note played), indicate both the correct duration and the correct octave.

---

357 After you have determined the mode, write the last note of this short melodic fragment. It will be the tonic.

Press PLAY

 (2)

ANSWER

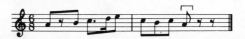

Singing the melody to yourself before making your response can be helpful. Be sure that your response was not only for A minor, but that it was an eighth-note duration and placed in the correct octave.

---

358 Indicate (1) the last note played and (2) the correct duration.

Press PLAY

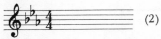 (2)

The performing instrument is_____ .

ANSWER

horn
If you made an error, listen to this frame again. Follow the printed music while doing so.

359 Follow the same procedure again in this frame.

Press PLAY

9:## 3/4 ――――――― (2)

The performing instrument is_____.

ANSWER

Anacrusis ⌐

bassoon
The *anacrusis* (upbeat or pickup) is a frequently used musical element. Sing this melody while conducting the metric beat.

---

360 In the next few frames, the printed music will differ rhythmically or melodically, or both rhythmically and melodically, from that which you hear. Bracket the measure where the difference occurs. On the second staff, write the notes which you hear for that measure. Be sure that the key signature corresponds with the mode played. This frame contains a rhythmic difference and a combination rhythm-pitch difference.

Press PLAY

(3)

ANSWER

361   Both melodic and pitch differences are found in this frame's melody. Locate points of difference and rewrite as before.

Press PLAY

(3)

The performing instrument is _____ .

ANSWER

cello
Rather than write in the accidentals, you need only change the key signature to make the printed music correspond to the minor mode played. The other differences are similar to ones encountered earlier in the program.

---

362   Sing this melody before listening. Locate points of difference while you compare your sung version with the played version. Rewrite as before.

Press PLAY

(3)

ANSWER

Starting note? Syncopation? Duration of tone? Review any areas in which you have difficulty.

363 The anacrusis mentioned in Frame 359 should not be a serious hearing problem, since the melodies in this program of study are introduced with a counting of the metric beat.

When a melody begins with an anacrusis, two measures will be counted as before, followed by a silent portion of the measure in which the anacrusis occurs. Maintain your conductor pattern during the silent portion of the measure in order to determine the precise rhythmic location of the anacrusis.

Listen to this example. Sing along with the second playing.

Press PLAY

Numbers and dots in parentheses indicate the metric beats and divisions.

(2)

ANSWER

Observe that the final measure has less than the full number of metric beats. As you perhaps already know, the missing beats are "borrowed" for the anacrusis. Sing this melody while conducting and tapping.

---

364 A portion of the beginning of this melody is omitted. The melody begins with an anacrusis. Complete the omitted portion.

Press PLAY

(3)

ANSWER

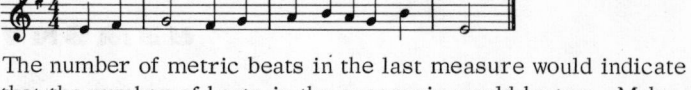

The number of metric beats in the last measure would indicate that the number of beats in the anacrusis would be two. Make use of this cue whenever possible.

---

365 Complete the omitted section.

Press PLAY

(3)

ANSWER

366 Follow the same procedure in this frame.

Press PLAY

The performing instrument is_____ .

(3)

ANSWER

piano

TEST 7
Before proceeding with the program, complete the test items for Test 7, which will be found at the back of the book. Obtain the tape-recorded materials for this test from your instructor.

367 All minor scales (natural, harmonic, and melodic) have the same pattern in the first five notes. The differences between these three forms of minor are found in the treatment of the sixth and seventh degrees.

The *natural* minor uses only notes indicated by its key signature. As a result, not only is the third degree a half step lower than the third degree in major, but the sixth and seventh degrees are a half step lower than those corresponding degrees in major.

Listen particularly to the sixth and seventh degrees (indicated by *) of this melody in G natural minor.

Press PLAY

(1)

The performing instrument is_____ .

ANSWER

clarinet

368   Notice the difference in sound between the last four notes of the B minor (natural minor) and its parallel B major scale. The difference will occur on the sixth and seventh degrees.

Press PLAY

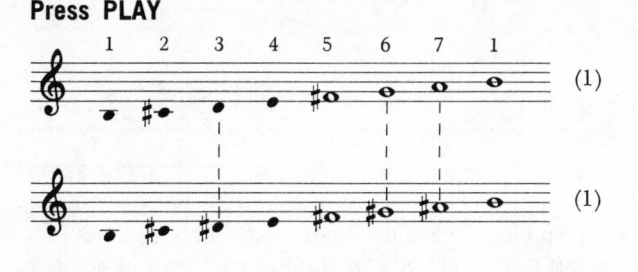

ANSWER

In natural minor the sixth and seventh are often referred to as *lowered* sixth and seventh degrees, because they sound lowered (and are lowered) in comparison with major.

---

369 **Press PLAY**

Another common form of minor is the *harmonic* minor. It differs from the natural minor in that the seventh degree is raised, creating a leading tone effect. Listen to this natural minor scale in A.

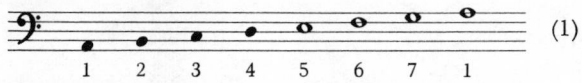

Now compare it in sound with the harmonic minor. Listen particularly to the upper tetrachord (upper four notes).

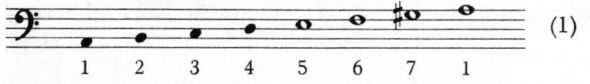

The performing instrument is_____.

ANSWER

bassoon

370 **Press PLAY**

Since the first five notes have the same pattern in all three common forms of minor, we can expect the differences which characterize a particular form to occur in the upper tetrachord. Compare the upper tetrachord of the natural minor scale in D with the upper tetrachord of the harmonic minor scale in D.

Natural minor

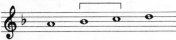

Observe the sound of the step-and-a-half interval (indicated by the sign ⌐⌐▲⌐⌐) in the harmonic minor.

Harmonic minor

The performing instrument is _____ .

ANSWER

trumpet

---

371 In the following frames, listen to the melodies comprised of notes from the upper tetrachords of minor scales. Indicate whether the melodies you hear are in natural minor or in harmonic minor, as in this example.

Press PLAY

This melody is _____ (natural, harmonic) minor. (2)

ANSWER

natural

---

372 Listen for the seventh degree. In this melody, it serves a leading-tone function.

Press PLAY

This melody is _____ (natural, harmonic) minor. (2)

ANSWER

harmonic

MELODIC PERCEPTION 152/153

373 Press PLAY

This melody is_____(natural, harmonic) minor. (2)

ANSWER

harmonic
If necessary, listen to the violin play this melody again. Sing this and accurately perform the one-and-a-half-step interval indicated.

---

374 Listen for the seventh degree in this melody. If it serves a leading-tone function (raised seventh) it is harmonic minor. If not, it is natural minor.

Press PLAY

This melody is_____(natural, harmonic) minor. (2)

ANSWER

natural

---

375 Occasionally, melodies will contain both natural and harmonic forms of the minor mode.

The next few frames will consist of melodies comprised of notes from the upper tetrachord of both natural and harmonic minor in combination. Mark the bracketed sections with H that are from the harmonic minor and with N that are from the natural minor, as in this example. The difference will occur on the seventh degree. Tap the beat as you listen.

Press PLAY

ANSWER

(1)

376 Mark the bracketed sections with H or with N to indicate the form of minor.
Sing the melody to yourself before writing your response.

Press PLAY

(2)

ANSWER

Have you noticed that the interval between the lowered sixth
and raised seventh in the harmonic minor sounds like an
interval skip? This can be a clue to identifying the harmonic
minor.

---

377 This melody contains notes in addition to those in the upper tetrachord.
Follow the same procedure.

Press PLAY

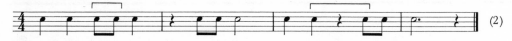

(2)

The performing instrument is_____ .

ANSWER

trombone

---

378 Follow the same procedure.

Press PLAY

(2)

ANSWER

379 In the next few frames, a portion of the melody will be omitted from the printed music. As you listen, determine if the omitted section is in harmonic or in natural minor. Above the omitted section, place either an H or an N, and then complete the omitted section, as in this example.

Press PLAY

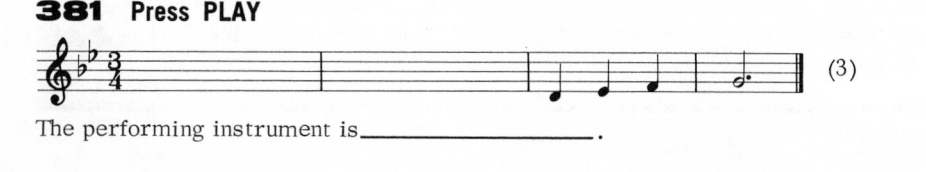
(1)

ANSWER

No written response required. Proceed to the next frame.

380 Indicate the form of minor used and complete the omitted section.
Press PLAY

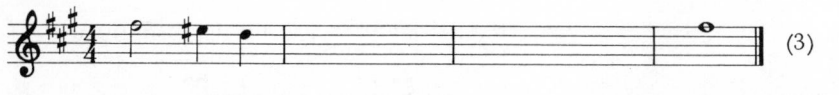
(3)

ANSWER

381 Press PLAY

(3)

The performing instrument is_____.

ANSWER

clarinet
Be aware of the feeling of a skip between the lowered sixth and raised seventh in harmonic minor (E flat and F sharp in this key).

382 Complete the omitted measures after determining the form of minor.
Press PLAY

(3)

ANSWER

---

383 **Press PLAY**

(3)

ANSWER

If you had difficulty hearing both the natural and the harmonic forms of minor in measure 2, carefully follow the printed music while you listen again. Check your final measure to be certain that the duration is accurately indicated.

---

384 In the following frames, locate and bracket points of difference. Write what is played on the second staff.
Press PLAY

(3)

ANSWER

Observe that the final seventh degree did not serve a leading-tone function.

385 Bracket points of difference and rewrite.
Press PLAY

(3)

The performing instrument is_____.

ANSWER

flute
Differences were of rhythm and pitch.

---

386 Locate the several points and types of difference and rewrite.
Press PLAY

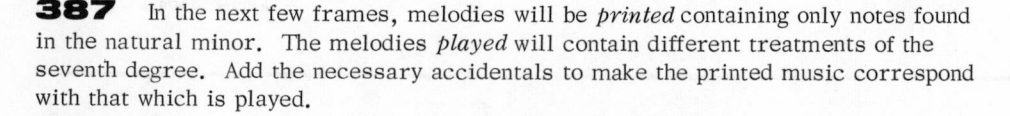

(3)

ANSWER

---

387 In the next few frames, melodies will be *printed* containing only notes found in the natural minor. The melodies *played* will contain different treatments of the seventh degree. Add the necessary accidentals to make the printed music correspond with that which is played.
Press PLAY

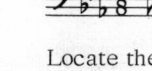

(3)

ANSWER

Locate the seventh degree before listening. Focus your attention on these points. If you hear a leading-tone effect, or if there is a step-and-a-half interval between the sixth and seventh, add the accidental which indicates a raised seventh.

388   Add the necessary accidentals.
Press PLAY

ANSWER

(3)

---

389   Follow the same procedure.
Press PLAY

(3)

ANSWER

---

390   Press PLAY

A third common form of minor is the *melodic* minor. The upper tetrachord of the melodic minor has two patterns:

1. An ascending pattern
2. A descending pattern

Observe the difference in pattern as you listen to this melodic minor scale.

(1)

The difference between the ascending and descending melodic minor is found on the _____ and_____ degrees.

ANSWER

sixth, seventh

391 Press PLAY

Listen to this natural minor scale. Compare it with the melodic minor scale.

Natural

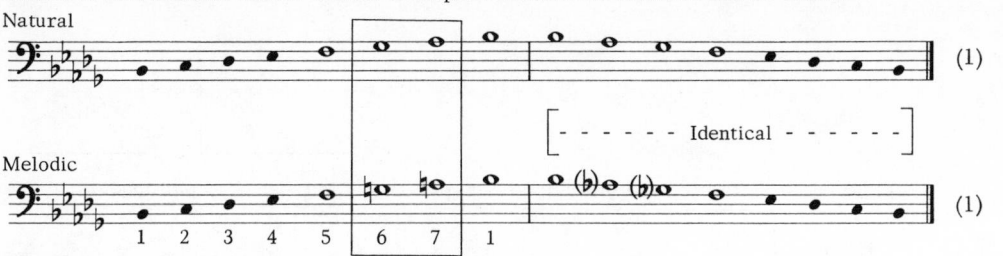

Notice how they are alike in the descending pattern.

The difference between the natural and melodic minor scale is found in the
_____ (ascending, descending) pattern.

ANSWER

ascending

---

392 Press PLAY

It was said earlier that the differences between the three forms of minor occur in
the upper tetrachord. In the *natural* minor, the sixth and seventh degrees are
lowered.

Natural

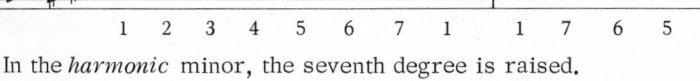

In the *harmonic* minor, the seventh degree is raised.

Harmonic

Look now at the correct answer.

ANSWER

Compare the *harmonic* minor scale with the *melodic* minor.

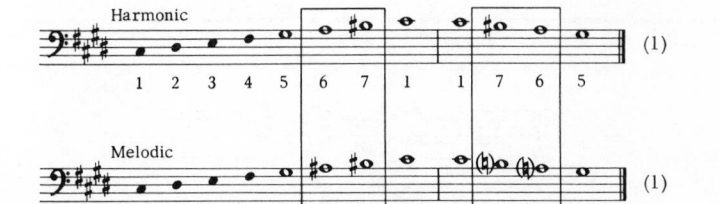

Stop the tape and sing the melodic minor scale, being careful
to sing a *raised* sixth and seventh ascending and a *lowered*
sixth and seventh *descending*.

393 In the next few frames, melodies comprised of notes from the upper tetrachord of minor scales will be played. Indicate whether the entire melody is in natural minor, in harmonic minor, or in melodic minor.

Press PLAY

This melody is in_____(natural, harmonic, melodic) minor. (2)

---

394 Since these melodies use only notes from the upper tetrachord, concentrate on the sixth and seventh degrees.

Press PLAY

This melody is in_____minor. (2)

Observe how the sound of the ascending upper tetrachord in melodic minor is the same as the upper tetrachord in major.

---

395 Indicate the form of minor.

Press PLAY

This melody is in_____minor. (2)

Notice that it was not until the third measure that the melody was defined as natural minor.

396 In the following frames, melodies will be comprised of notes from one of the three complete forms of minor scales, rather than limited only to the upper tetrachord of the minor scales.

Press PLAY

This melody is in _____ minor. (2)

ANSWER

melodic

Sing this melody. Notice the similarity of the final two measures to a major modality.

397 **Press PLAY**

This melody is in _____ minor. The performing instrument is
_____ . (2)

ANSWER

harmonic

violin

398 In the next few frames, melodies will be printed using notes found in the natural minor scale. Minor melodies will be played using one or a combination of the three forms of minor. Add the necessary accidentals which will make the printed music correspond to that which is played.

Press PLAY

(3)

The performing instrument is _____ .

ANSWER

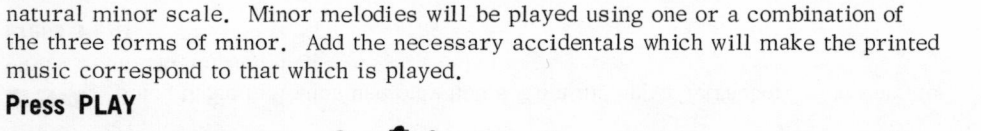

flute

First of all, the melody should have been recognized as being ascending melodic minor. Having done so, it was necessary only to raise the sixth and seventh degrees. Always sing the melodies before proceeding to the next frame.

399 Follow the same procedure. Focus your attention on the sixth and seventh degrees.

Press PLAY

 (3)

ANSWER

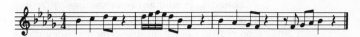

Only the third and fourth measures contained the sixth and seventh degrees. In neither measure did the trumpet play them raised.

400 This melody is comprised of two forms of minor.

Press PLAY

 (3)

ANSWER

Be alert to the leading-tone effect in measures 2 and 4 while you sing this melody.

401 Add the necessary accidentals.

Press PLAY

 (3)

ANSWER

402 Add the necessary accidentals.

Press PLAY

 (3)

ANSWER

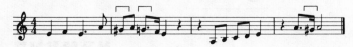

403   In the following frames, melodies will be comprised of notes from the complete octave in minor keys. A section of the printed melody will be omitted.

Indicate with N (natural), H (harmonic), or M (melodic) the type of minor played in the omitted section, as in this example. If more than one are used in the omitted section, put MN, MHN, etc.

Complete the omitted section, as in this example.

Press PLAY

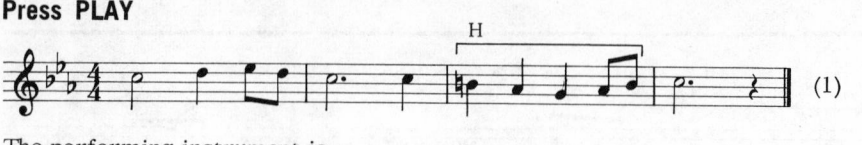

(1)

The performing instrument is_____.

ANSWER

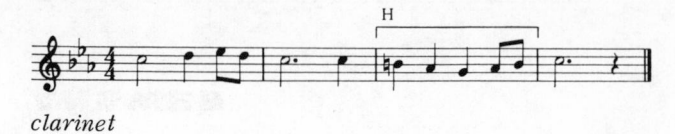

clarinet

---

404   Determine the form (or forms) of minor used in the omitted section. After listening to the melody, sing it before making your response.

Press PLAY

 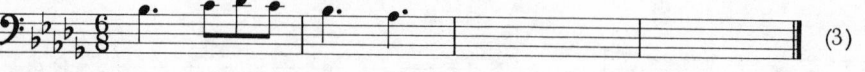

(3)

ANSWER

---

405   **Press PLAY**

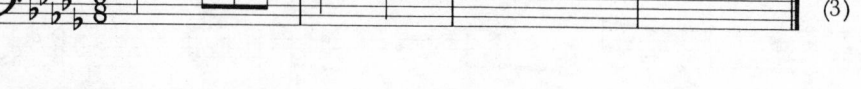

(3)

The performing instrument is_____.

ANSWER

cello

If you had difficulty with the first omitted note, sing the descending skip of 3 (minor) *down* to 5. Do this several times. Listen again to the tape if necessary.

406 Press PLAY

(3)

ANSWER

---

407 Listen for two distinct forms of minor.
Press PLAY

(3)

ANSWER

---

408 Write this minor melody.
Press PLAY

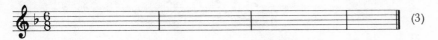

(3)

ANSWER

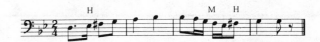

---

409 Press PLAY

(3)

ANSWER

410   In the following frames the printed melody will differ from that which you hear. Bracket the points of difference and rewrite. Differences will be rhythmic or melodic. Making use of N, H, or M in your first listening (to indicate the form of minor) may be an aid to you.

Press PLAY

(3)

The performing instrument is_____ .

ANSWER

horn
The two points of difference involved the starting note and the raised sixth in melodic minor. Sing this melody again.

---

411   Sing this melody before listening. While singing, be conscious of the tonal center. Compare what you sing (what is printed) with what is played. Notice that the melody ends on the dominant.

Press PLAY

(3)

The performing instrument is _____ .

ANSWER

cello
If you made errors, carefully examine the nature of them. Be alert for similar problems in future frames. Sing the corrected melody.

412 Both syncopation and a form of minor are involved in differences in this frame.

Press PLAY

(3)

The performing instrument is_____ .

ANSWER

trombone
Always listen enough times to be confident of your response, but attempt to accomplish each response with as few hearings as possible.

---

413 Locate and rewrite points of difference.

Press PLAY

(3)

ANSWER

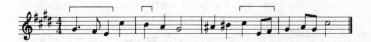

TEST 8
Before proceeding with the program, complete the test items for Test 8, which will be found at the back of the book. Obtain the tape-recorded materials for this test from your instructor.

414 Press PLAY

Until this point in the program, all interval skips have been between tones in the tonic triad. Interval skips also occur between tones other than those in the tonic triad. Some interval skips may be identified as a result of repetition of a portion of the melody, as in this example.

(1)

ANSWER

Observe that the skip was between the fourth and seventh degrees. However, rather than the interval skip, it was the repetition which was obvious. Writing the repetition would automatically have taken care of the interval skip.

---

415 The omitted section contains an interval skip as a result of exact repetition.

Press PLAY

(3)

ANSWER

Notice that if you recognize a section as an *exact* repetition, it is only necessary to "copy" that section. Continue to be alert to the form of minor.

---

416 Press PLAY

(3)

The performing instrument is_____ .

ANSWER

trombone

417 This frame involves exact repetition, but with a different application.

Press PLAY

 (3)

Measure 3 is a repetition of measure 2, except that measure 2 was omitted in your response item. Your response also needed an interval skip between the first and third degrees. Sing this melody.

---

418 Notice the skip within the repeated pattern in this frame.

Press PLAY

 (3)

The performing instrument is _____.

horn

---

419 This melodic fragment ends on the dominant. The omitted section contains a melodic pattern and its repetition.

Press PLAY

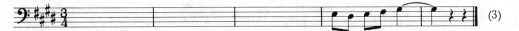 (3)

420 Occasionally, a repeated pattern will vary in a few points in its repeated form and yet be similar enough to the original form to be identified as a repetition. This is called *altered repetition.*

Listen to the illustration of altered repetition in this frame. The original pattern is indicated by the closed bracket, A⌐――――⌐, and its altered repetition is indicated by the open-end bracket, A¹⌐――――.

(1)

The performing instrument is_____.

ANSWER

trumpet

The alteration in the repeated form of the pattern may be either rhythmic or melodic, or it may be both rhythmic and melodic. However, the pitch of the first note of the altered repetition will be the same as that of the original form.

The first pattern will usually have an obvious metric or rhythmic identification; for example, the illustration in this frame had a pattern beginning on beat 1 of a measure.

---

421 Complete the omitted section. It contains an altered repetition of the second measure.

Press PLAY

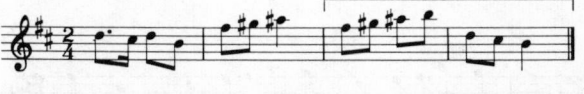

(3)

ANSWER

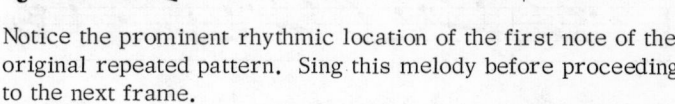

Notice the prominent rhythmic location of the first note of the original repeated pattern. Sing this melody before proceeding to the next frame.

---

422 **Press PLAY**

(3)

ANSWER

423 Measure 3 is an altered repetition of measure 2.

Press PLAY

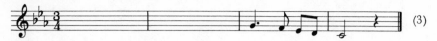 (3)

ANSWER

The pitches of measures 2 and 3 were the same. If you have difficulty with the rhythm, *always* be sure to conduct the metric beats and tap the divided beats.

---

424 Be alert for rests in this melody.

Press PLAY

 (3)

ANSWER

Any problems with the 3-5 skip in measure 2? If so, pay particular attention to this interval while you sing the melody again.

---

425 Both the original and the altered form of the repetition are omitted. Listen for the rhythmic prominence of the patterns.

Press PLAY

 (3)

The performing instrument is _____.

ANSWER

flute

426   The repeated pattern in this major melody will not begin on beat 1.
Press PLAY

(3)

The performing instrument is _____ .

ANSWER

bassoon
Notice how important it is to maintain the feeling of the beats while you listen. Doing so can facilitate perception of the repetition. The next frame contains a similar use of the repeated pattern.

427   The repeated pattern in this melody begins with an anacrusis (pickup) effect. (Be aware that only a portion of the second measure is printed.) Complete the omitted section.
Press PLAY

(3)

The performing instrument is _____ .

ANSWER

piano

428   **Press PLAY**

(3)

ANSWER

If you are having difficulty with repeated patterns, review Frames 414 to 428 before proceeding.

429 Try to sing this melody accurately after two hearings. After you can sing it, write it.

Press PLAY

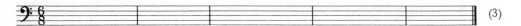

(3)

ANSWER

ANSWER

Starting note? 1-5 skip in measure 2? Altered repetition of measure 3? 5-1 skip to final note? Review any problems before continuing.

---

430 In the next few frames, the printed music will differ from that played. Differences may involve *any* of the concepts studied thus far in minor melodies. Give particular attention to repetition. Locate points of difference and rewrite.

Press PLAY

(3)

ANSWER

---

431 **Press PLAY**

(3)

ANSWER

Melodic minor? Rhythm? Listen as many times as necessary but attempt to complete your response with three or less hearings.

432 Press PLAY

(3)

ANSWER

Octave inversion? Rhythm? Durations? Continue to conduct and tap while listening and singing.

433 Press PLAY

(3)

ANSWER

* Notice both rhythmic and pitch differences.

434 Examine the printed music carefully before listening. Include singing as a part of your examination.

Press PLAY

(3)

ANSWER

Listen to this again if you made errors or had difficulty. Conduct and sing along with the piano.

435 Few composers restrict themselves to using the various forms of minor in a strict way. As a result, melodies are found with the altered sixth and seventh degrees occurring in all sorts of combinations.

Listen to this melody. Observe the sound of the upper tetrachord with the different sixth and seventh degree usage.

1. Unaltered seventh, raised sixth
2. Melodic minor
3. Natural minor
4. Raised sixth and seventh descending
5. Unaltered sixth

Press PLAY

The performing instrument is _____.

ANSWER

cello

---

436 In the next few frames, you will have a melody printed in natural minor. The melody you hear will have the sixth and seventh altered in various combinations.

1. Locate all sixth and seventh degrees with brackets.
2. Mark L (lowered) or R (raised), according to what you hear at each of the indicated points.
3. Write in the appropriate accidentals for the form of minor you indicate.

Follow this example.

Press PLAY

Printed:

Your response:

ANSWER

Reminder: Locate and bracket the sixth and seventh degrees on the music prior to listening. While listening, focus your attention on these notes.

437 Add the appropriate accidentals.
Press PLAY

(3)

ANSWER

---

438 Follow the same procedure.
Press PLAY

(3)

The performing instrument is _____.

ANSWER

clarinet
While singing this melody, notice how the final two measures sound like the upper tetrachord of major.

---

439 Add necessary accidentals.
Press PLAY

(3)

The performing instrument is _____.

ANSWER

violin

---

440 **Press PLAY**

(3)

ANSWER

441 Listen for the treatment of the sixth and seventh degrees.
Press PLAY

 (3)

The performing instrument is _____ .

ANSWER

horn
Indications of treatment of sixth and seventh will no longer be included in the correct answer other than in the musical notation. You may find it helpful to continue the practice, however.

---

442 Complete the omitted section.
Press PLAY

 (3)

ANSWER

The lowered seventh followed by a raised sixth is sometimes confused with the descending melodic minor. If you had this problem, sing the descending melodic minor and compare it with the clarinet line in the second measure. The next frame contains a similar problem.

---

443 **Press PLAY**

 (3)

ANSWER

444 Press PLAY

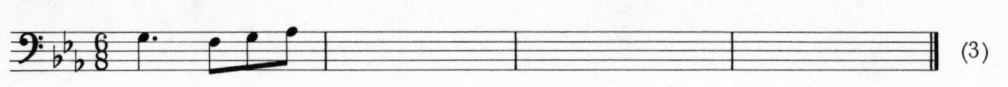 (3)

ANSWER

ANSWER

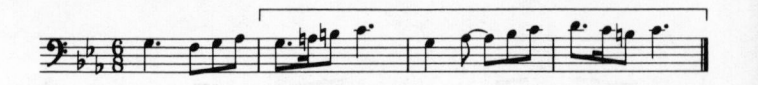

---

445 Write this melody.

Press PLAY

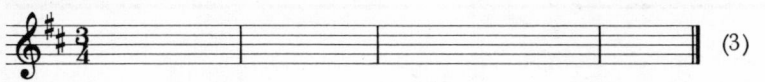 (3)

ANSWER

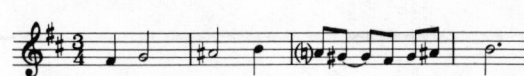

Compare accidentals carefully. If you have had difficulty with Frames 435 to 445, review this section again before proceeding.

TEST 9

Before proceeding with the program, complete the test items for Test 9, which will be found at the back of the book. Obtain the tape-recorded materials for this test from your instructor.

446 The next frames will contain melodies in *major* mode. Your responses may involve any of the rhythmic or pitch concepts studied thus far.

Press PLAY

 (3)

ANSWER

Remember to sing the melodies *before* making your response and again *after* you have checked your response with the correct answer. Conduct the metric beats and tap the divisions while listening and while singing.

447 Complete the omitted section.

Press PLAY

 (3)

Rest? Durations? Repetitions? Octave skip? Listen to this frame again if necessary.

---

448 Be careful to maintain tonal center while listening (leading-tone effect, notes of tonic triad). Complete omitted section.

Press PLAY

 (3)

Starting note? Octave skip? Rhythm? Correct any errors before proceeding.

---

449 The melodic fragment in this frame does not end on the tonic. Complete the omitted measures.

Press PLAY

 (3)

---

450 This melody contains hemiola.

Press PLAY

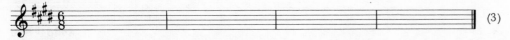 (3)

The performing instrument is_____.

violin

451 Write this melody.

Press PLAY

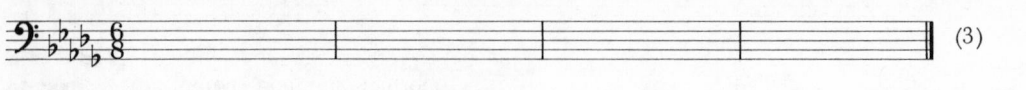

(3)

ANSWER

---

452 Write this melody

Press PLAY

(3)

The performing instrument is _____.

ANSWER

horn
If you have had difficulty with Frames 446 to 452, go over these again before proceeding.

---

453 Write this melody.

Press PLAY

(3)

ANSWER

(The syncopated figure in measure 2 could have been written

.)

454 Compare the printed melody with the performance in the next few frames. Locate differences and rewrite as before.

Press PLAY

(3)

ANSWER

---

455 Follow the same procedure.

Press PLAY

(3)

ANSWER

---

456 Follow the same procedure.

Press PLAY

(3)

ANSWER

457 In the remainder of the book, both major and minor melodies will be played. In each of the following frames, the first perception task will be to determine modality (major or minor).

In the next few frames melodies will be printed but key signatures will be omitted. Tonality will be indicated for each. After listening, determine modality.

Fill in the appropriate key signature. If in minor, add the necessary accidentals wherever the sixth and seventh degrees are raised.

Press PLAY

F _____   (3)

ANSWER

F minor

As early as the third note, you should have determined the modality to be minor. Always spot the notes which give the clue to modality (third and in this frame sixth and seventh).

---

458 Supply the correct key signature.

Press PLAY

C _____   (3)

ANSWER

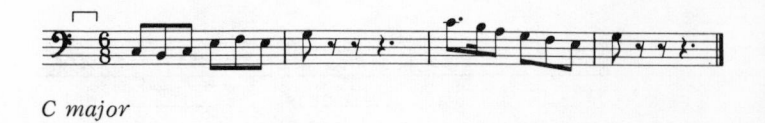

C major

---

459 Follow the same procedure.

Press PLAY

D _____   (3)

ANSWER

D minor

* Not until the appearance of the minor third degree could you be sure that it was minor. Because of the raised sixth and seventh it is melodic minor.

460 Write this melody. It does not end on the tonic.
Press PLAY

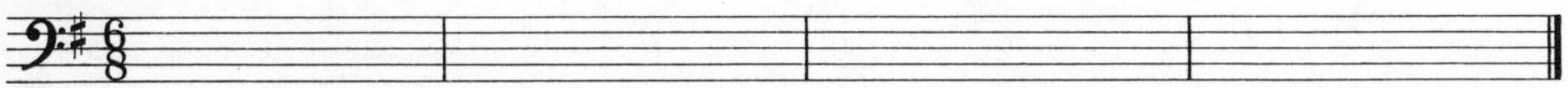

ANSWER

(3)

The performing instrument is _____ .

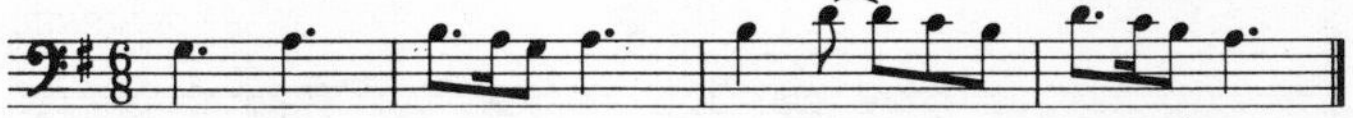

cello

---

461 Write this melody.
Press PLAY

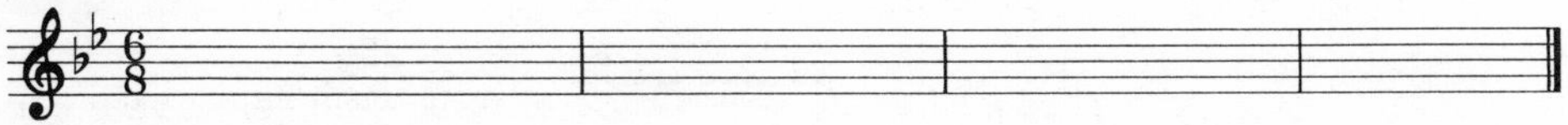

ANSWER

(3)

The performing instrument is _____ .

clarinet

---

462 Press PLAY

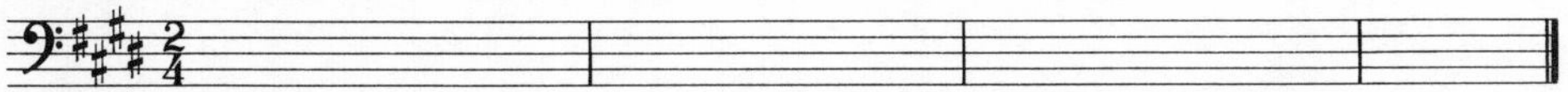

ANSWER

(3)

The performing instrument is _____ .

piano

---

463 Press PLAY

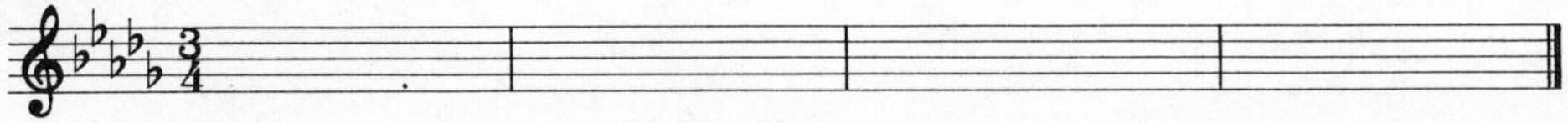

ANSWER

(3)

The performing instrument is _____ .

horn

464 Press PLAY

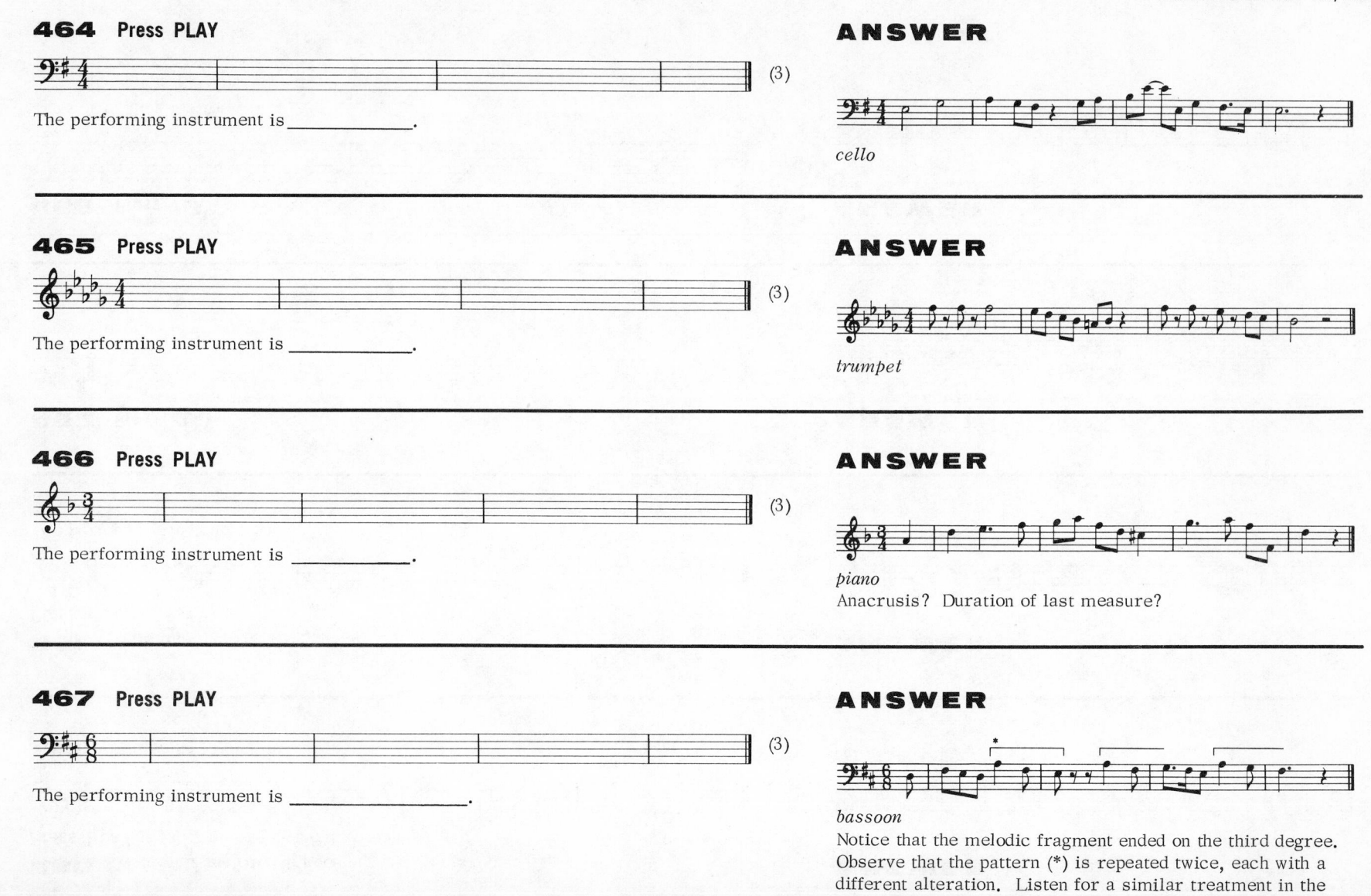

The performing instrument is _____.

ANSWER

cello

465 Press PLAY

The performing instrument is _____.

ANSWER

trumpet

466 Press PLAY

The performing instrument is _____.

ANSWER

piano

Anacrusis? Duration of last measure?

467 Press PLAY

The performing instrument is _____.

ANSWER

bassoon

Notice that the melodic fragment ended on the third degree.
Observe that the pattern (*) is repeated twice, each with a
different alteration. Listen for a similar treatment in the
next frame.

468 Press PLAY

The performing instrument is _____ .

ANSWER

trombone

---

469 Thus far, all repeated patterns have immediately followed the original. Repetition of a pitch pattern may also be delayed because of interpolated material, as in this example.

Press PLAY

The performing instrument is _____ .

ANSWER

flute
This melody illustrates a delayed-altered repetition. Obviously, an exact repetition may also be delayed.

---

470 Listen for delayed repetition.
Press PLAY

The performing instrument is _____ .

ANSWER

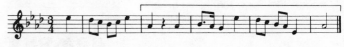

violin

---

471 Press PLAY

The performing instrument is _____ .

ANSWER

trumpet

472 Press PLAY

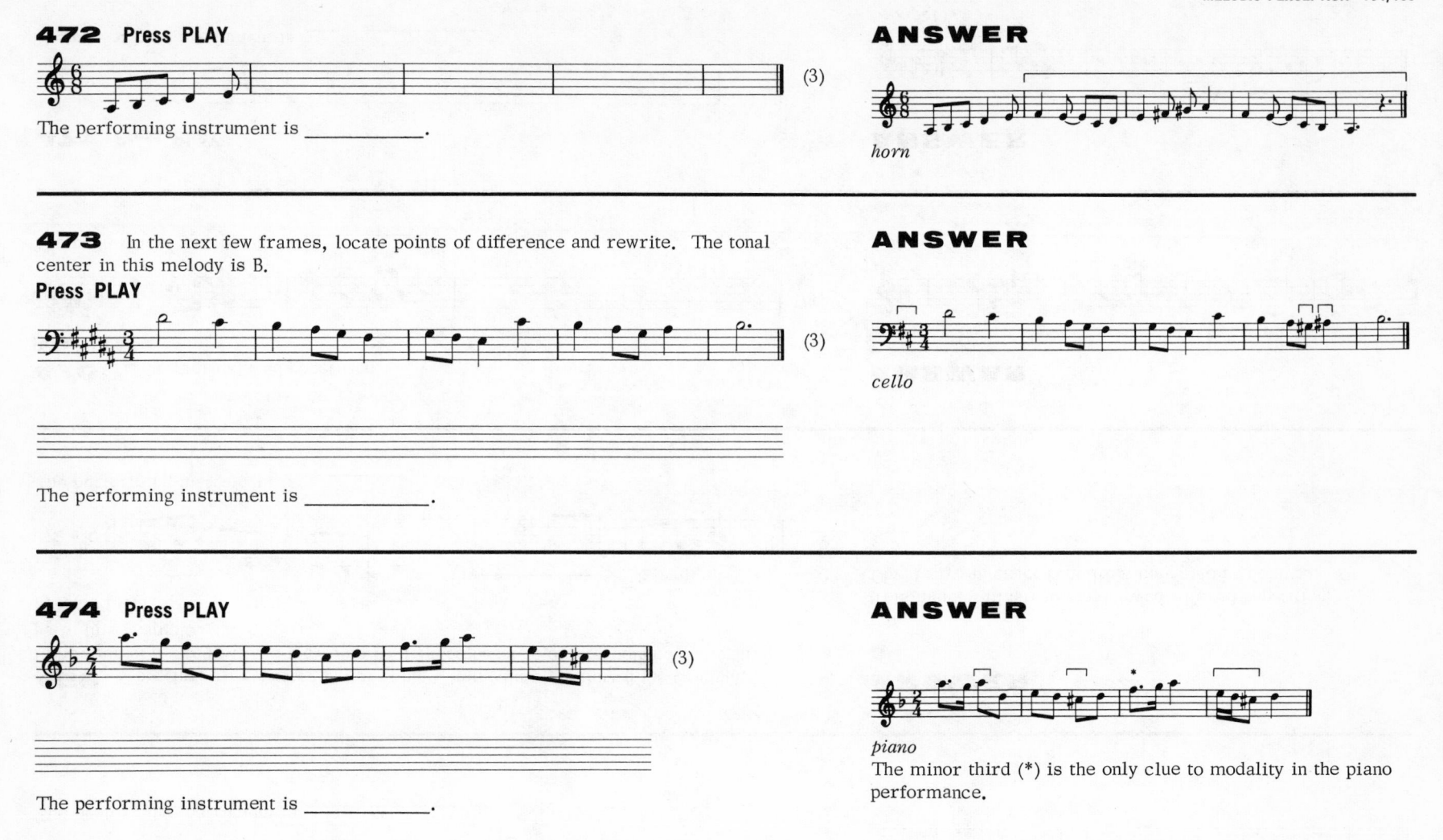

The performing instrument is _____.

ANSWER

horn

473

In the next few frames, locate points of difference and rewrite. The tonal center in this melody is B.

Press PLAY

(3)

The performing instrument is _____.

ANSWER

cello

474 Press PLAY

(3)

The performing instrument is _____.

ANSWER

piano

The minor third (*) is the only clue to modality in the piano performance.

475 **Press PLAY**

(3)

The performing instrument is _____.

ANSWER

bassoon

---

476 This melody does not end on the tonic.
Press PLAY

(3)

The performing instrument is _____.

ANSWER

piano

---

477 Occasionally, composers will move back and forth between major and minor in one melody. To some extent the different alterations of the sixth and seventh degrees imply this major-minor vacillation.

Confirmation of movement between modalities is obtained when the *third* degree is altered. When it is "lowered," the modality is minor. When it is "raised," modality is major. Listen to this melody which involves both modes.

Press PLAY

(1)

ANSWER

trumpet
Bracket the thirds before listening. Indicate with L (lower) or R (raised) the types as you listen. After you have done this, add accidentals. Do the same for sixth and seventh degrees if necessary.

478 All key signatures for the next few frames indicate major. Add accidentals to make the third correspond to minor *when* the performance indicates it.
Press PLAY

The performing instrument is _____ .

(3)

ANSWER

trombone

479 Add appropriate accidentals.
Press PLAY

The performing instrument is _____ .

(3)

ANSWER

flute

480 **Press PLAY**

The performing instrument is _____ .

(3)

ANSWER

violin

481 **Press PLAY**

The performing instrument is _____ .

(3)

ANSWER

bassoon

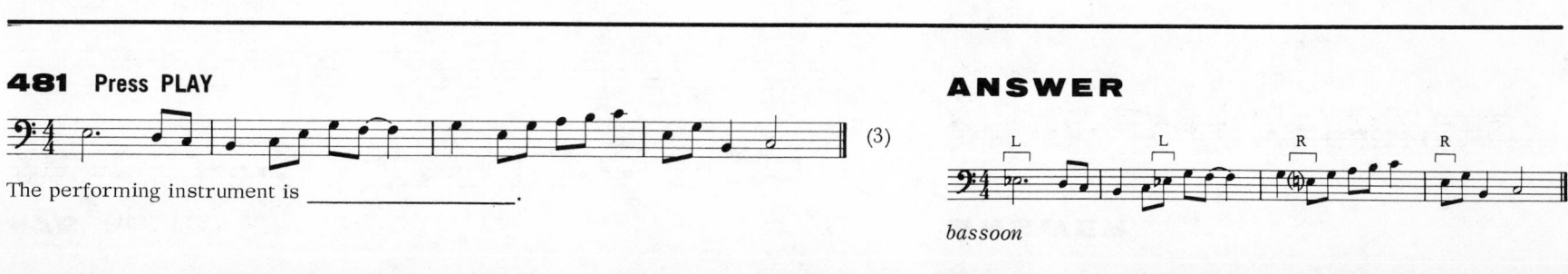

482 The printed music will differ from that played. Locate the points of
difference and rewrite as before.

Press PLAY

(3)

The performing instrument is _____ .

ANSWER

trombone

---

483 **Press PLAY**

(3)

The performing instrument is _____ .

ANSWER

cello

---

484 **Press PLAY**

(3)

The performing instrument is _____ .

ANSWER

horn

485 In the next frames, complete the omitted sections. Listen for the type of third contained in the omitted sections.

Press PLAY

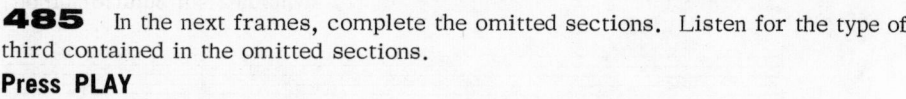

(3)

The performing instrument is _____.

ANSWER

clarinet

---

486 **Press PLAY**

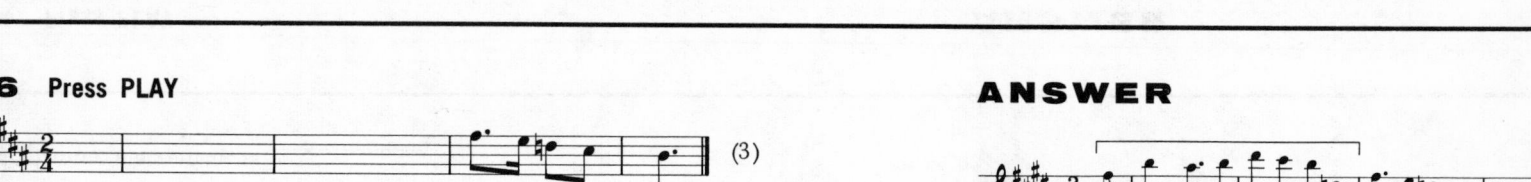

(3)

The performing instrument is _____.

ANSWER

flute

---

487 **Press PLAY**

(3)

The performing instrument is _____.

ANSWER

trombone

---

488 The final note is other than the tonic.

Press PLAY

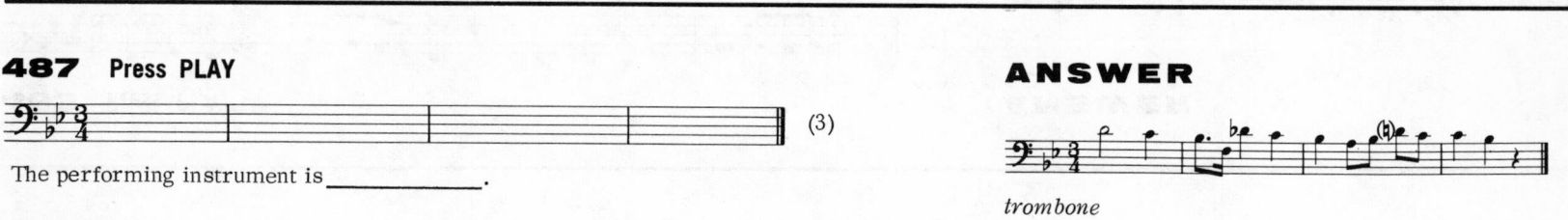

(3)

The performing instrument is _____.

ANSWER

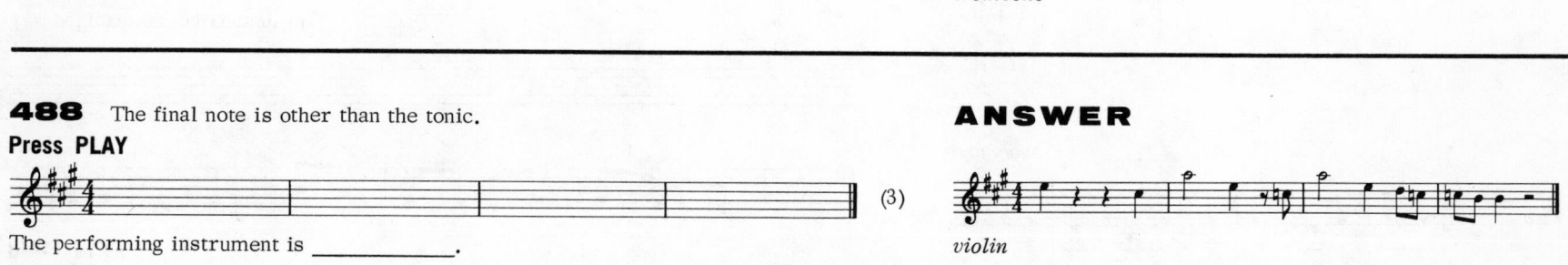

violin

489 Press PLAY

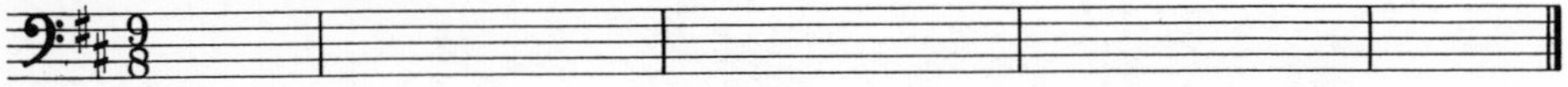

The performing instrument is _____.

ANSWER

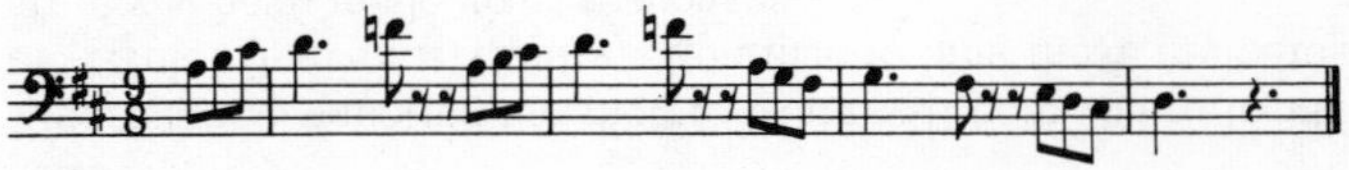

bassoon

---

490 Listen for a shift of accent within the repeated figure.
Press PLAY

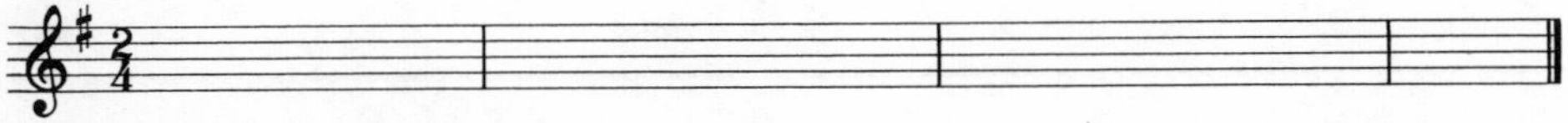

The performing instrument is _____.

ANSWER

clarinet

---

491 Press PLAY

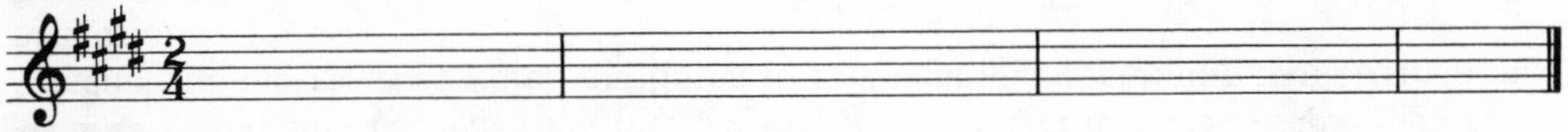

The performing instrument is _____.

ANSWER

piano

---

492 Press PLAY

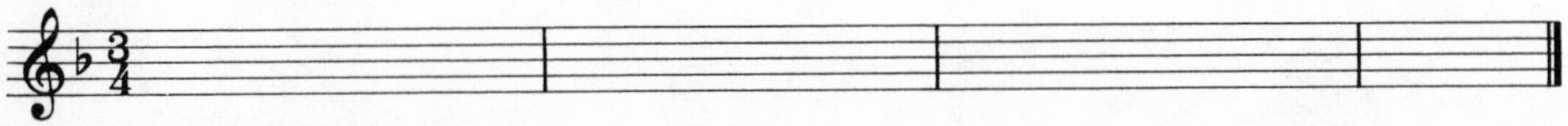

The performing instrument is _____.

ANSWER

trumpet

If you have had difficulty with alterations of the third (moving back and forth between major and minor), review Frames 477 to 492 before proceeding.

TEST 10
Before proceeding with the program, complete the test items for Test 10, which will be found at the back of the book. Obtain the tape-recorded materials for this test from your instructor.

493 Another frequent rhythmic pattern is the *triplet* found in simple meter. Conduct the metric beat while you listen to this example containing triplet rhythmic patterns.
Press PLAY

(1)

The performing instrument is _____ .

ANSWER

horn
A triplet is a group of three notes, or their equivalent, used in the place of two notes of equal value. A figure 3 is always used with the triplet, for example,  . The effect is that of superimposing compound meter on simple meter.

494 Complete the omitted section.
Press PLAY

(3)

The performing instrument is _____ .

ANSWER

cello
Vigorously conducting the metric beats will help you to locate the triplet figure metrically. Continue to sing these melodies after you have made your responses.

495 **Press PLAY**

(3)

The performing instrument is _____.

ANSWER

flute

496 **Press PLAY**

(3)

The performing instrument is _____.

ANSWER

trombone

497 **Press PLAY**

(3)

The performing instrument is _____.

ANSWER

violin
Take notice of the difference in sound between ♩♩♩ and
♩♩♩ (*). Sing this melody while vigorously conducting the
metric beats.

498 Press PLAY

The performing instrument is _____.

ANSWER

piano

499 Press PLAY

The performing instrument is _____.

ANSWER

clarinet

500 Press PLAY

The performing instrument is _____.

ANSWER

trumpet

501 Press PLAY

The performing instrument is _____.

ANSWER

bassoon

502 Press PLAY

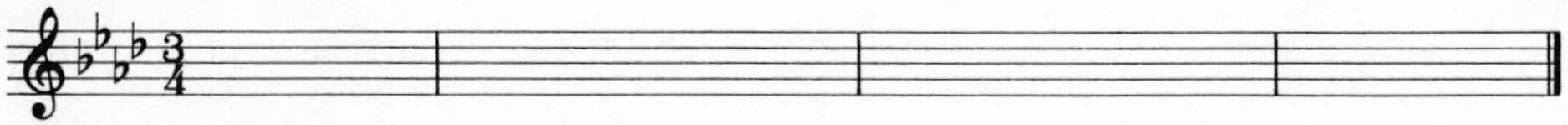

The performing instrument is _____ .

ANSWER

(3)

horn

---

503 Press PLAY

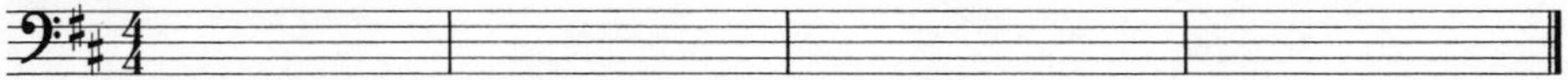

The performing instrument is _____ .

ANSWER

(3)

cello

---

504 Press PLAY

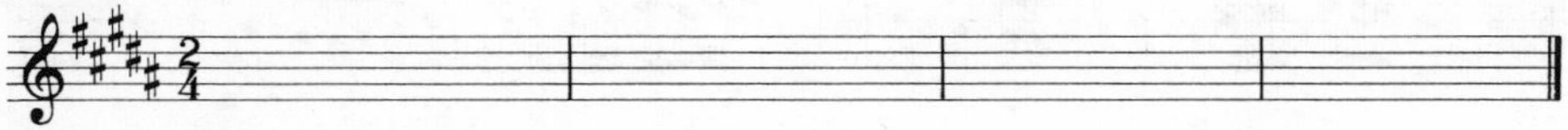

The performing instrument is _____ .

ANSWER

(3)

flute

---

505 In the next frames, locate differences and rewrite.
Press PLAY

ANSWER

(3)

piano

The performing instrument is _____ .

506 Press PLAY

The performing instrument is _____.

(3)

ANSWER

clarinet

507 Press PLAY

The performing instrument is _____.

(3)

ANSWER

bassoon

508

A rhythmic pattern similar in concept to the triplet figure is the *duplet* found in compound meter. Conduct the metric beat while you listen to this example containing duplet rhythmic patterns.

Press PLAY

The performing instrument is _____.

(1)

ANSWER

violin

A duplet is a group of two notes, or their equivalent, used in the place of three notes of equal value. A figure 2 is always used with the duplet, for example, . The effect is that of superimposing simple meter on compound meter.

509 In the next frames, complete the omitted section.

Press PLAY

The performing instrument is _____.

(3)

ANSWER

trumpet

510 **Press PLAY**

The performing instrument is _____.

(3)

ANSWER

horn

511 **Press PLAY**

The performing instrument is _____.

(3)

ANSWER

trombone

512 **Press PLAY**

The performing instrument is _____.

(3)

ANSWER

cello

513 Press PLAY

The performing instrument is _____.

ANSWER

flute

514 Press PLAY

The performing instrument is _____.

ANSWER

piano

515 Press PLAY

The performing instrument is _____.

ANSWER

trumpet

516 Press PLAY

The performing instrument is _____.

ANSWER

bassoon

517 Press PLAY

The performing instrument is _____.

(3)

ANSWER

horn

---

518 Press PLAY

The performing instrument is _____.

(3)

ANSWER

cello

---

519 Press PLAY

The performing instrument is _____.

(3)

ANSWER

clarinet

---

520 In this frame and the next, locate differences and rewrite.
Press PLAY

(3)

The performing instrument is _____.

ANSWER

trombone

521 **Press PLAY**

(3)

The performing instrument is _____ .

ANSWER

violin

TEST 11
Before proceeding with the program, complete the test items for Test 11, which will be found at the back of the book. Obtain the tape-recorded materials for this test from your instructor.

522 The remainder of the book will consist of additional practice melodies comprised of the melodic elements presented in this program of study. No new melodic concepts will be introduced.

The response section will consist of a staff, key signature, meter signature, bar lines, and a place to indicate the performing instrument. The correct answer will be printed in the right column, as before. On each frame:
1. Press PLAY when you are ready to listen.
2. Conduct the metric beat and tap the divisions while listening.
3. Sing the melody to yourself before writing your response.
4. Check your written response with the correct answer.
5. Correct any errors.
6. Sing the correct melody again before proceeding to the next frame.

ANSWER

Proceed now to Frame 523.

523 Press PLAY

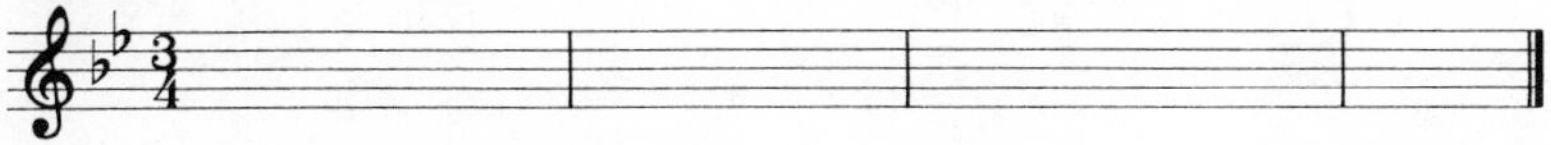

The performing instrument is _____ . (3)

ANSWER

flute

---

524 Press PLAY

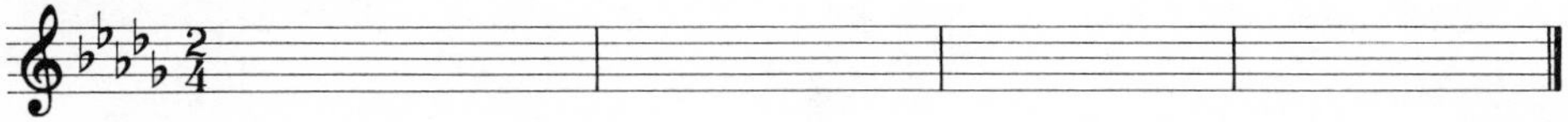

The performing instrument is _____ . (3)

ANSWER

horn

---

525 Press PLAY

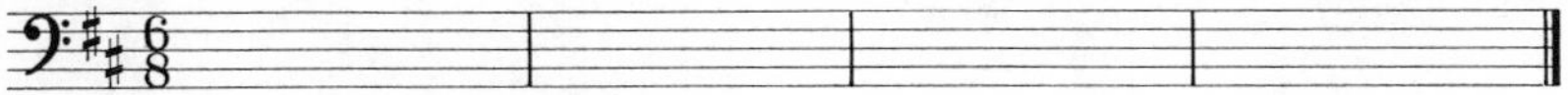

The performing instrument is _____ . (3)

ANSWER

bassoon

---

526 Press PLAY

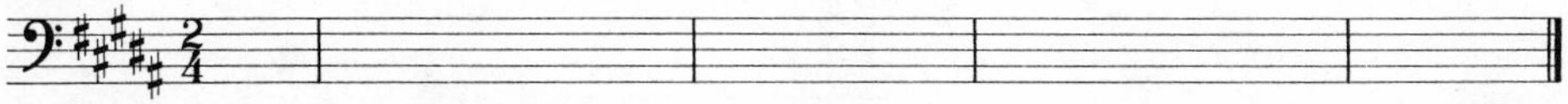

The performing instrument is _____ . (3)

ANSWER

cello

527 Press PLAY

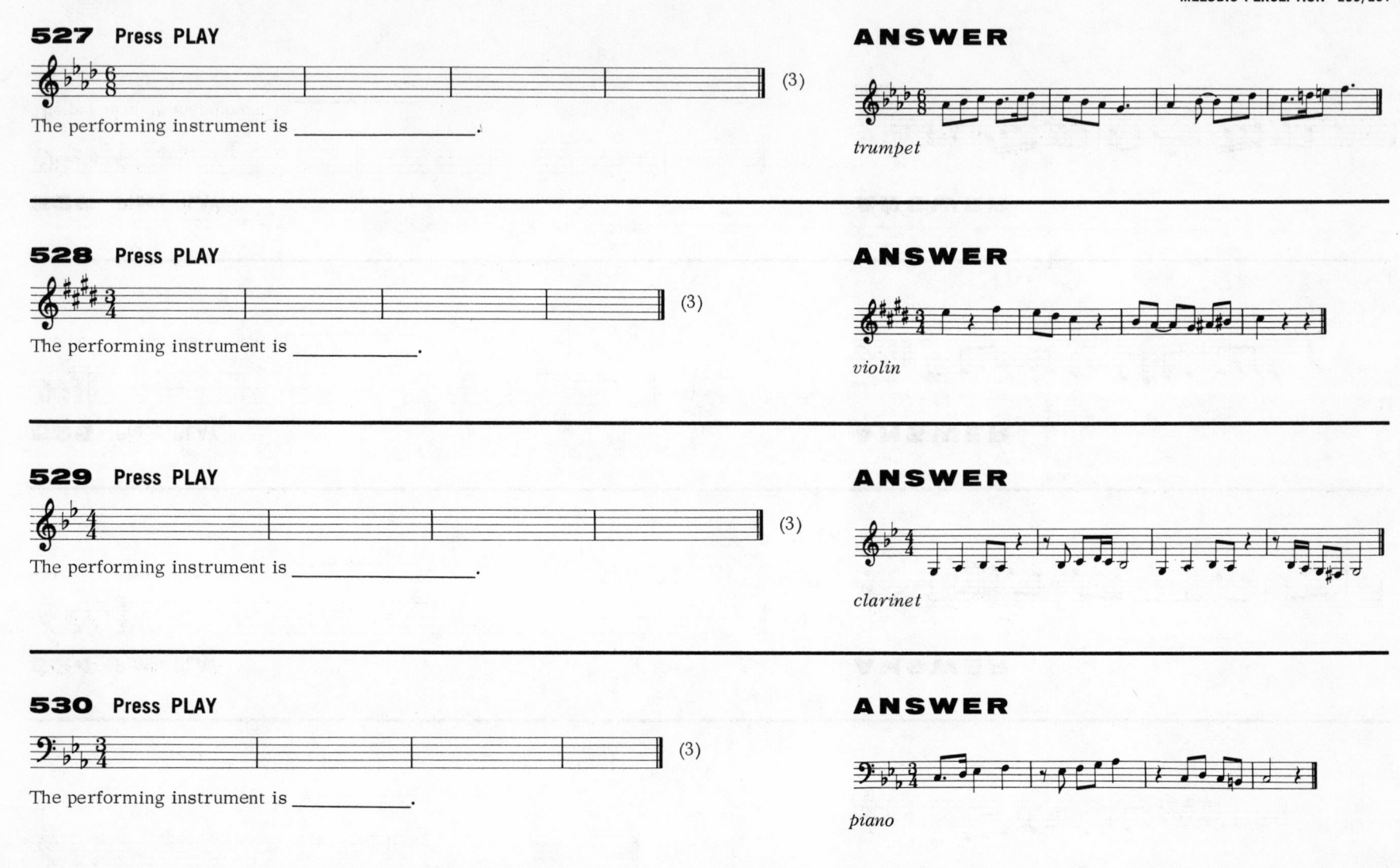

The performing instrument is _____.

ANSWER

trumpet

528 Press PLAY

The performing instrument is _____.

ANSWER

violin

529 Press PLAY

The performing instrument is _____.

ANSWER

clarinet

530 Press PLAY

The performing instrument is _____.

ANSWER

piano

531 **Press PLAY**

 (3)

The performing instrument is _____ .

ANSWER

trombone

---

532 **Press PLAY**

(3)

The performing instrument is _____ .

ANSWER

clarinet

---

533 **Press PLAY**

(3)

The performing instrument is _____ .

ANSWER

violin

---

534 **Press PLAY**

(3)

The performing instrument is _____ .

ANSWER

piano

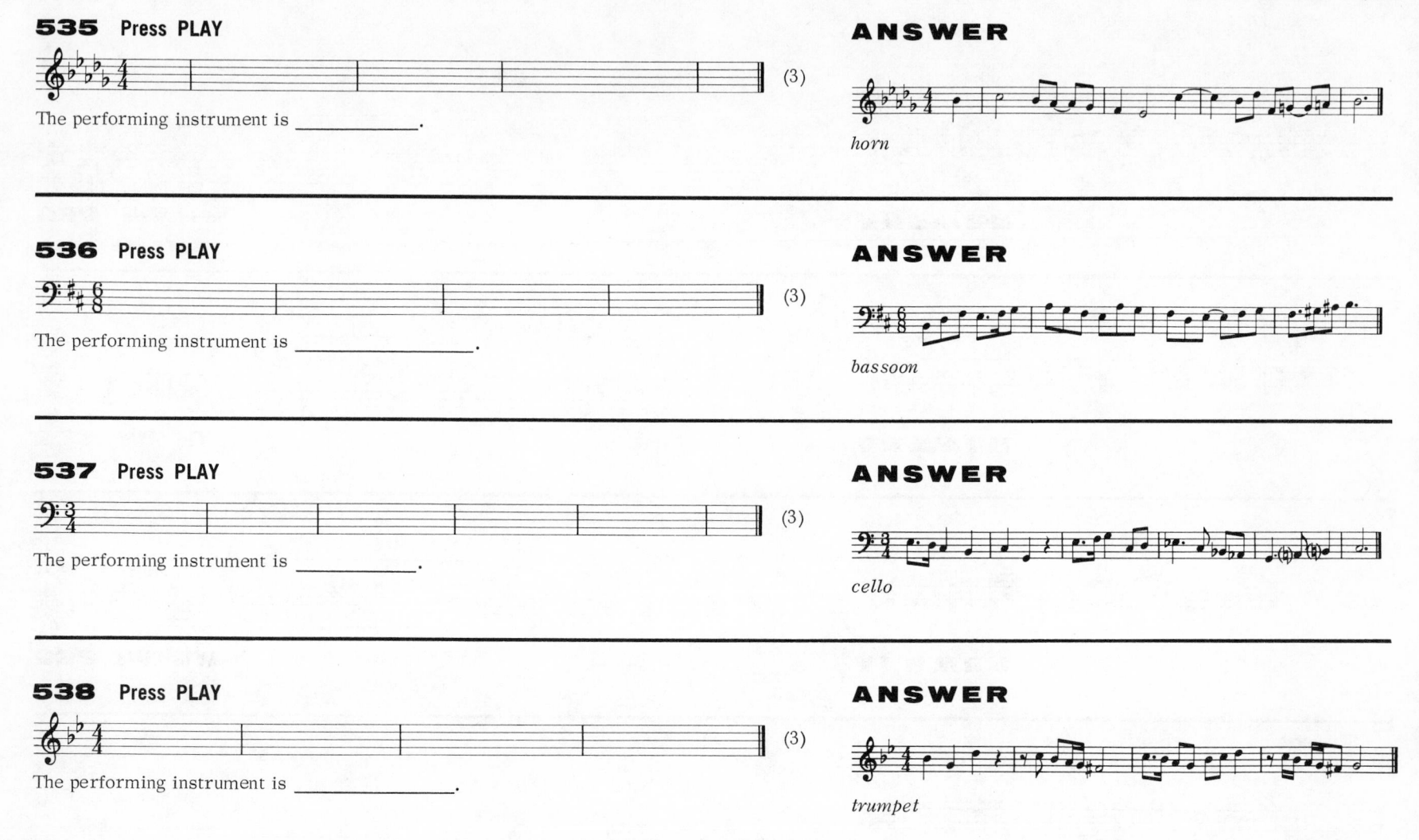

535 Press PLAY

The performing instrument is _____.

(3)

ANSWER

horn

536 Press PLAY

The performing instrument is _____.

(3)

ANSWER

bassoon

537 Press PLAY

The performing instrument is _____.

(3)

ANSWER

cello

538 Press PLAY

The performing instrument is _____.

(3)

ANSWER

trumpet

539 The final measure is incomplete.
Press PLAY

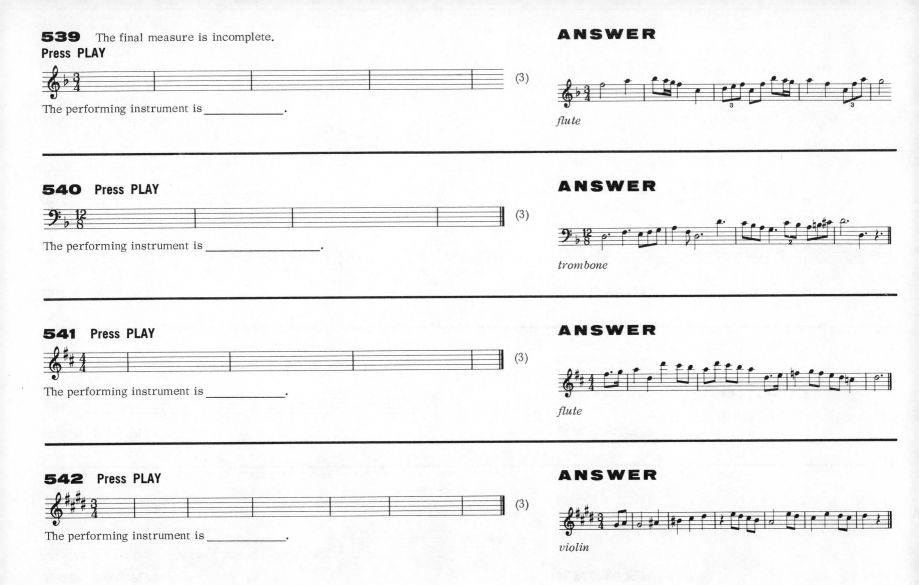

The performing instrument is _____.

ANSWER

flute

---

540 Press PLAY

The performing instrument is _____.

ANSWER

trombone

---

541 Press PLAY

The performing instrument is _____.

ANSWER

flute

---

542 Press PLAY

The performing instrument is _____.

ANSWER

violin

543 Press PLAY

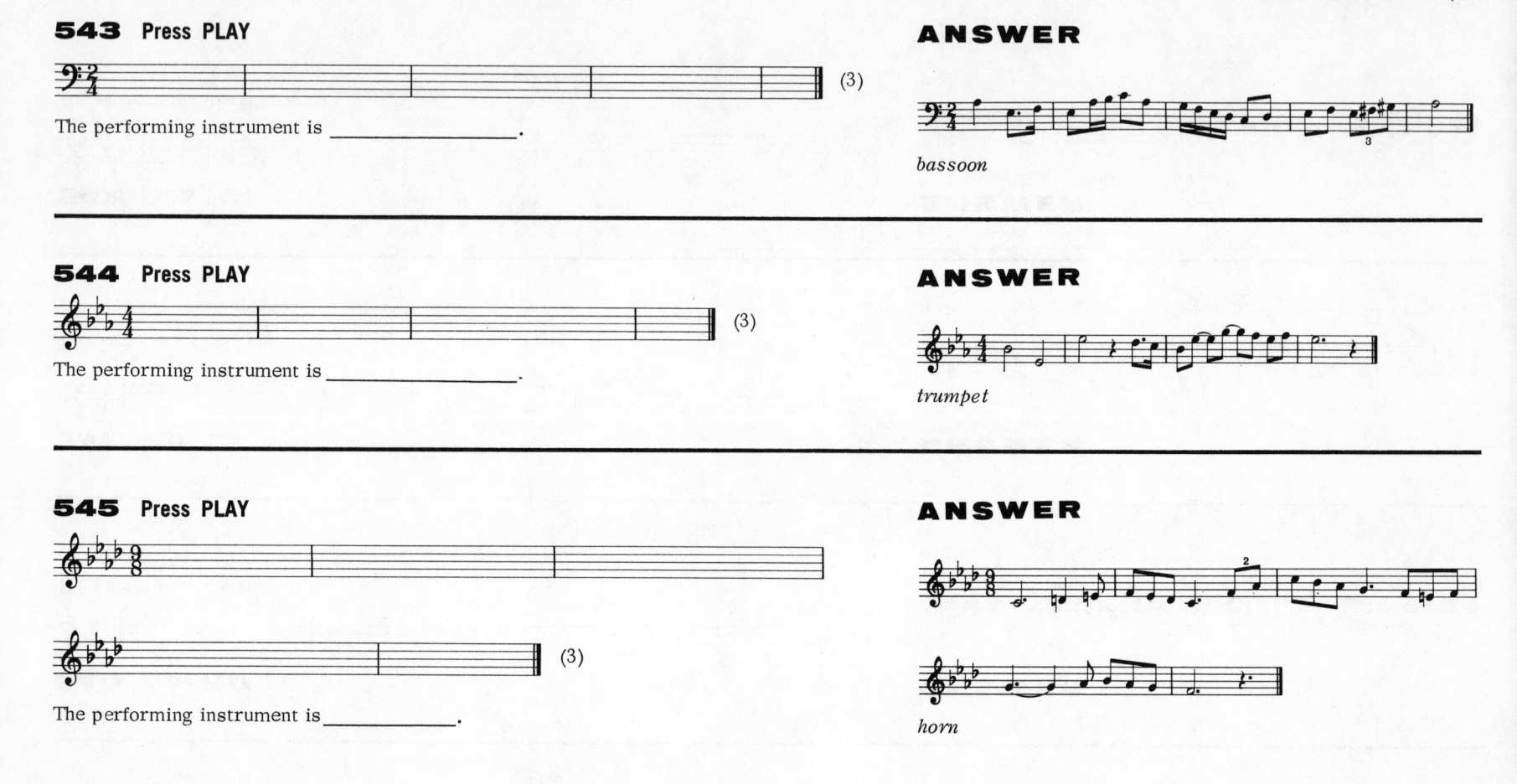

(3)

The performing instrument is _____.

ANSWER

bassoon

544 Press PLAY

(3)

The performing instrument is _____.

ANSWER

trumpet

545 Press PLAY

(3)

The performing instrument is _____.

ANSWER

horn

546 Press PLAY

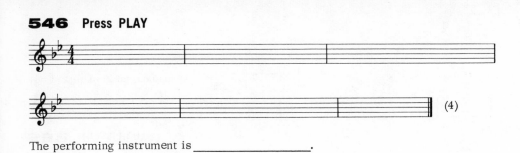

The performing instrument is _____.

ANSWER

clarinet

---

547 Press PLAY

The performing instrument is _____.

ANSWER

piano

---

548 Press PLAY

The performing instrument is _____.

ANSWER

trombone

549 Press PLAY

The performing instrument is _____.

ANSWER

cello

550 Press PLAY

The performing instrument is _____.

ANSWER

flute

551 Press PLAY

The performing instrument is _____.

ANSWER

cello

552 Press PLAY

The performing instrument is _____.

ANSWER

trumpet

553 Press PLAY

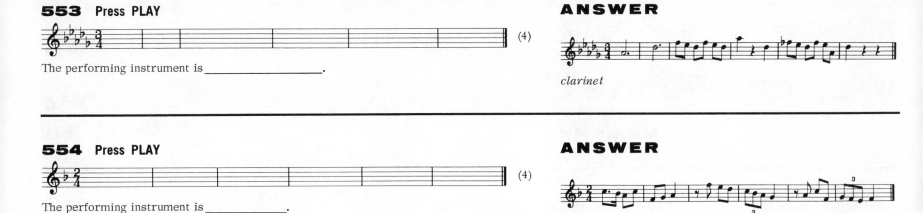

The performing instrument is _____.

ANSWER

clarinet

554 Press PLAY

The performing instrument is _____.

ANSWER

piano

555 Press PLAY

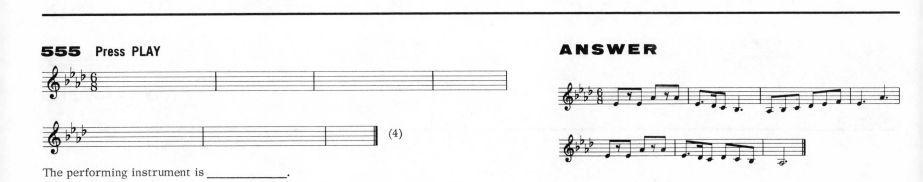

The performing instrument is _____.

ANSWER

horn

556 Press PLAY

The performing instrument is _____.

ANSWER

horn

557 Press PLAY

The performing instrument is _____.

ANSWER

violin

558 Press PLAY

The performing instrument is _____.

ANSWER

trombone

559 Press PLAY

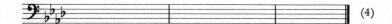
(4)

The performing instrument is _____.

ANSWER

trumpet

---

560 Press PLAY

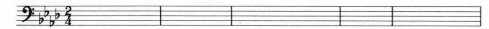

(4)

The performing instrument is _____.

ANSWER

bassoon

---

561 Press PLAY

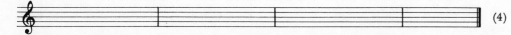
(4)

The performing instrument is _____.

ANSWER

flute

562 **Press PLAY**

The performing instrument is _____.

ANSWER

trombone

563 **Press PLAY**

The performing instrument is _____.

ANSWER

horn

564 **Press PLAY**

The performing instrument is _____.

ANSWER

cello

565 Press PLAY

The performing instrument is _____.

ANSWER

violin

---

566 Press PLAY

The performing instrument is _____.

ANSWER

piano

---

567 Press PLAY

The performing instrument is _____.

ANSWER

bassoon

568 Press PLAY

The performing instrument is _____.

ANSWER

trumpet

569 Press PLAY

The performing instrument is _____.

ANSWER

clarinet

570 Press PLAY

The performing instrument is _____.

ANSWER

flute

TEST 12 (Final)

Complete the test items for Test 12, which will be found at the back of the book.

Obtain the tape-recorded materials for this test from your instructor.

CONDUCTOR BEAT PATTERNS

Duple pattern

$\dfrac{2}{4} \quad \dfrac{6}{8}$

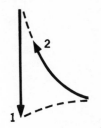

Triple pattern

$\dfrac{3}{4} \quad \dfrac{9}{8}$

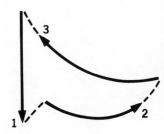

Quadruple pattern

$\dfrac{4}{4} \quad \dfrac{12}{8}$

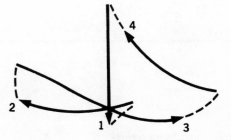

SELF-ANALYSIS CHART
Section I, Frames 1 to 68

Frame	Nature of error	Remarks

SELF-ANALYSIS CHART
Section II, Frames 69 to 117

Frame	Nature of error	Remarks

SELF-ANALYSIS CHART

Section III, Frames 118 to 166

Frame	Nature of error	Remarks

SELF-ANALYSIS CHART

Section IV, Frames 167 to 241

Frame	Nature of error	Remarks

SELF-ANALYSIS CHART

Section V, Frames 242 to 285

Frame	Nature of error	Remarks

SELF-ANALYSIS CHART

Section VI, Frames 286 to 319

Frame	Nature of error	Remarks

SELF-ANALYSIS CHART

Section VII, Frames 320 to 366

Frame	Nature of error	Remarks

SELF-ANALYSIS CHART

Section VIII, Frames 367 to 413

Frame	Nature of error	Remarks

SELF-ANALYSIS CHART
Section IX, Frames 414 to 445

Frame	Nature of error	Remarks

SELF-ANALYSIS CHART

Section X, Frames 446 to 492

Frame	Nature of error	Remarks

SELF-ANALYSIS CHART
Section XI, Frames 493 to 521

Frame	Nature of error	Remarks

SELF-ANALYSIS CHART
Section XII, Frames 522 to 570

Frame	Nature of error	Remarks

TEST 1

1. Bracket points of difference between what is printed and what is played. On the second staff, write what is played at the points of difference.

2. Complete the omitted section.

3. Bracket points of difference between what is printed and what is played. On the second staff, write what is played at the points of difference.

4. Complete the omitted section.

5. Write this melody.

TEST 2

1. Using arrows, indicate the rhythmic location of melodic direction change.

2. Bracket points of difference between what is printed and what is played. On the second staff, write what is played at the points of difference.

3. Complete the omitted section.

4. Complete the omitted section.

5. Write this melody.

TEST 3

1. Complete the omitted section.

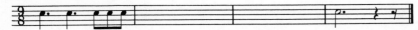

The performing instrument is _____.

2. Complete the omitted section.

The performing instrument is _____.

3. Complete the omitted section

The performing instrument is _____.

4. Complete the omitted section.

The performing instrument is _____.

5. Write this melody.

The performing instrument is _____.

TEST 4

1. Bracket points of difference between what is printed and what is played. On the second staff, write what is played at the points of difference.

The performing instrument is _____.

2. Complete the omitted section.

The performing instrument is _____.

3. Write this melody.

The performing instrument is _____.

4. Complete the omitted section.

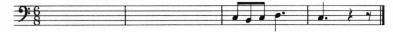

The performing instrument is _____.

5. Write this melody.

The performing instrument is _____.

TEST 5 (Midcourse)

1. Complete the omitted section.

The performing instrument is _____.

2. Bracket points of difference between what is printed and what is played. On the second staff, write what is played at the points of difference.

The performing instrument is _____.

3. Complete the omitted section.

The performing instrument is _____.

4. Write this melody.

The performing instrument is _____.

5. Bracket points of difference between what is printed and what is played. On the second staff, write what is played at the points of difference.

The performing instrument is _____.

6. Write this melody.

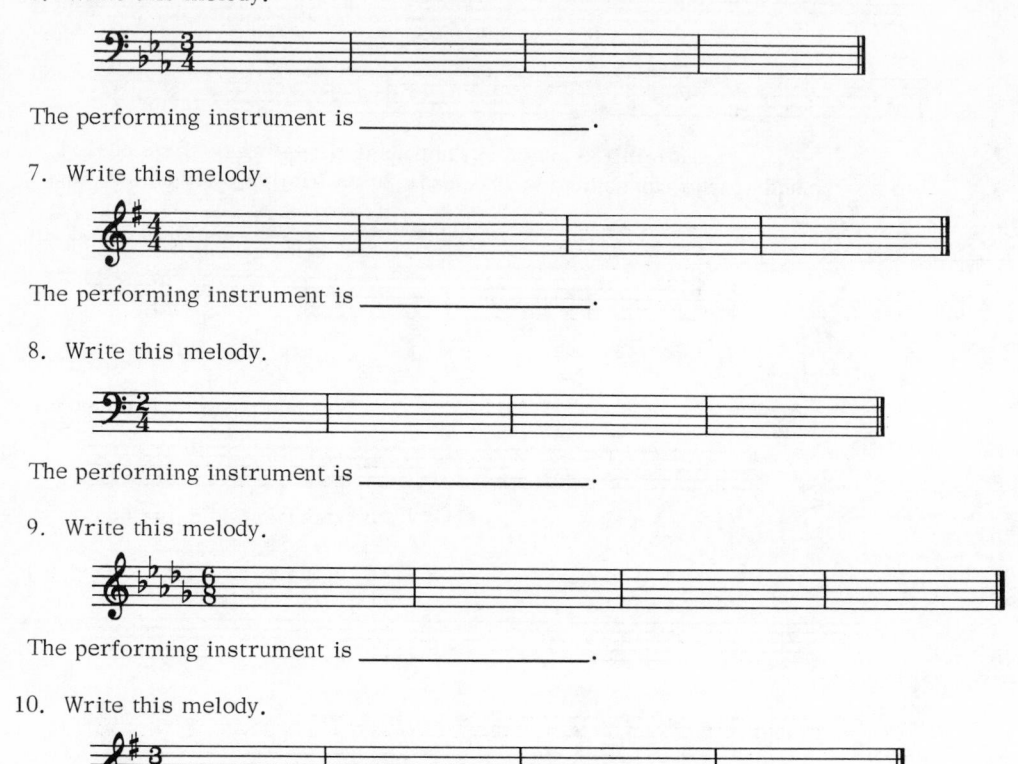

The performing instrument is _____.

7. Write this melody.

The performing instrument is _____.

8. Write this melody.

The performing instrument is _____.

9. Write this melody.

The performing instrument is _____.

10. Write this melody.

The performing instrument is _____.

TEST 6

1. Complete the omitted section.

The performing instrument is _____.

2. Bracket points of difference between what is printed and what is played. On the second staff, write what is played at the points of difference.

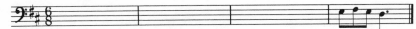

The performing instrument is _____.

3. Complete the omitted section.

The performing instrument is _____.

4. Write this melody.

The performing instrument is _____.

5. Write this melody.

The performing instrument is _____.

TEST 7

Indicate in items 1, 2, and 3 whether the melody played is major or minor. The final note will be the tonic. Underline the correct answer.

1. Major, minor   (2)

2. Major, minor   (2)

3. Major, minor   (2)

4. Complete the omitted section.

5. Complete the omitted section.

6. Bracket points of difference between what is printed and what is played. On the second staff, write what is played at the points of difference.

7. Write this melody.

TEST 8

In test items 1 and 2, minor melodies will be printed using only notes found in the natural minor scale. Add the appropriate accidentals which will make the printed music correspond with that which is played.

1.

2.

3. Bracket points of difference between what is printed and what is played. On the second staff, write what is played at the points of difference.

4. Complete the omitted section.

5. Write this melody.

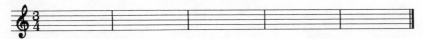

6. Write this melody.

TEST 9

1. Complete the omitted section.

The performing instrument is _____.

2. Write this melody.

The performing instrument is _____.

3. Write this melody.

The performing instrument is _____.

4. Add the appropriate accidentals which will make the printed music correspond with that which is played.

The performing instrument is _____.

5. Add the appropriate accidentals which will make the printed music correspond with that which is played.

The performing instrument is _____.

6. Write this melody.

The performing instrument is _____.

TEST 10

1. Complete the omitted section.

The performing instrument is _____.

2. Write this melody.

The performing instrument is _____.

3. Write this melody.

The performing instrument is _____.

4. Bracket points of difference between what is printed and what is played. On the second staff, write what is played at the points of difference.

The performing instrument is _____.

5. Write this melody.

The performing instrument is _____.

TEST 11

1. Bracket points of difference between what is printed and what is played. On the second staff, write what is played at the points of difference.

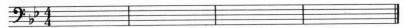

The performing instrument is _____.

2. Write this melody.

The performing instrument is _____.

3. Bracket points of difference between what is printed and what is played. On the second staff, write what is played at the points of difference.

The performing instrument is _____.

4. Write this melody.

The performing instrument is _____.

5. Write this melody.

The performing instrument is _____.

1. Write this melody.

The performing instrument is _____.

2. Write this melody.

The performing instrument is _____.

3. Bracket points of difference between what is printed and what is played. On the second staff, write what is played at the points of difference.

The performing instrument is _____.

4. Write this melody.

The performing instrument is _____.

5. Write this melody.

The performing instrument is _____.

6. Write this melody.

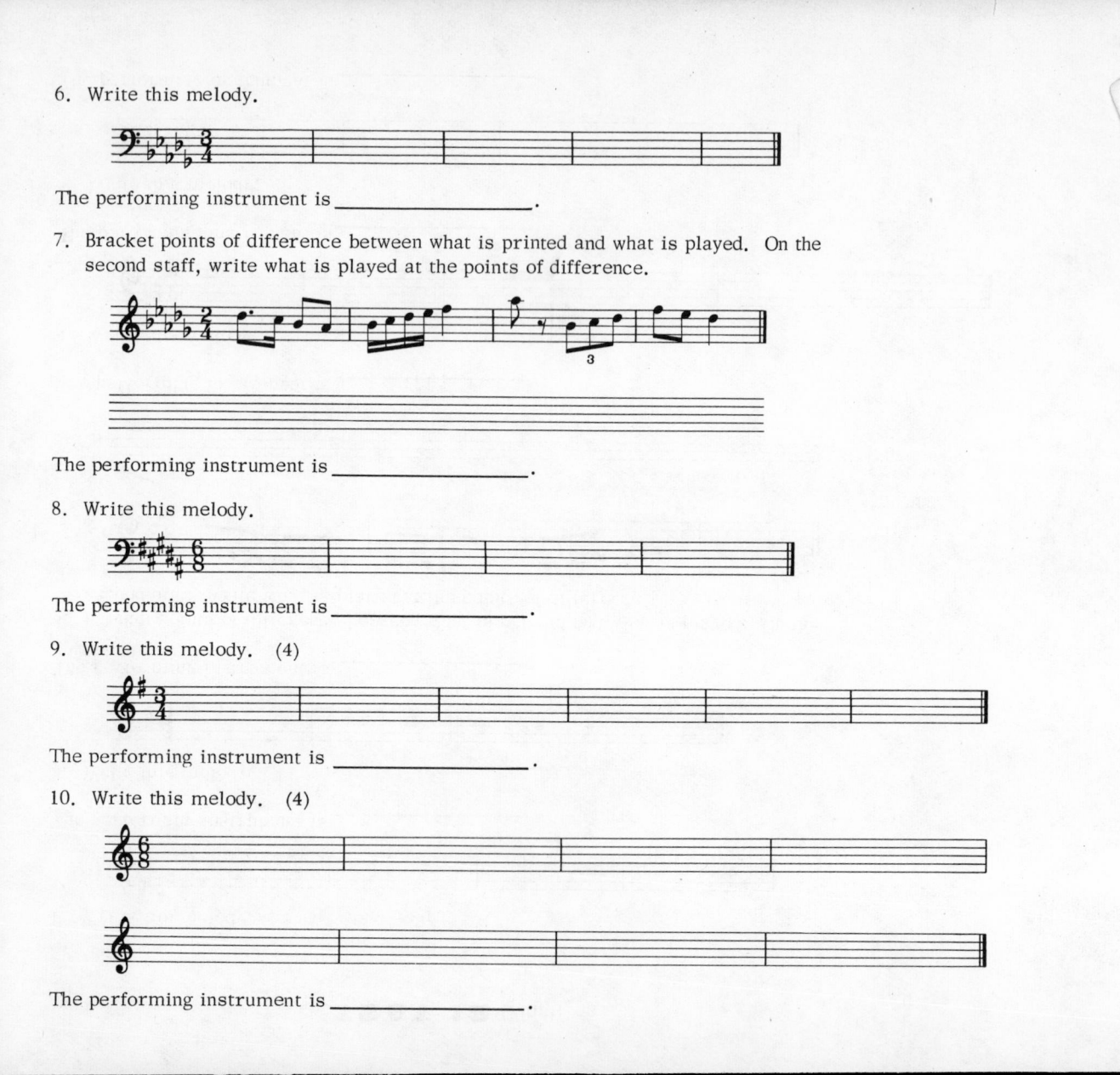

The performing instrument is _____.

7. Bracket points of difference between what is printed and what is played. On the second staff, write what is played at the points of difference.

The performing instrument is _____.

8. Write this melody.

The performing instrument is _____.

9. Write this melody. (4)

The performing instrument is _____.

10. Write this melody. (4)

The performing instrument is _____.